ACCIDENTS IN NORTH AMERICAN MOUNTAINEERING

VOLUME 8 • NUMBER 1 • ISSUE 54

2001

THE AMERICAN ALPINE CLUB
GOLDEN

THE ALPINE CLUB OF CANADA
BANFF

ISSN   0065-082X

ISBN   0-930410-90-4

Manufactured in Canada

Published by
The American Alpine Club, Inc.
710 Tenth Street, Suite 100
Golden, CO 80401

Cover Illustration
The photo is of the fracture line of the avalanche in Glory Bowl that killed Joel Roof (28) on December 1. You can see his snowboard track going into the fracture at the top center. One can also see the two Wyoming Transportation Dept. Gaz-Ex blasters that set off explosions of propane and oxygen by remote control in order to provoke avalanches when the road is clear. They are on the back cover and cast long shadows. They had not been used the morning of the avalanche because they were broken. Photographed by Angus M. Thuermer, Jr., for the *Jackson Hole* (WY) *News*.

CONTENTS

SAFETY COMMITTEES 2000

ACCIDENTS IN
NORTH AMERICAN MOUNTAINEERING
Fifty-Fourth Annual Report of the Safety Committees
of The American Alpine Club and The Alpine Club of Canada

This is the fifty-fourth issue of *Accidents in North American Mountaineering* and the twenty-third issue in which The Alpine Club of Canada has contributed data and narratives.

Canada: This was a year in which an unusually high number of experienced climbers were involved in serious accidents in Canada. Many of these were preventable, but some were situations in which the only thing the person could have done differently was to stay at home and read a book. These accidents are reminders that not all risks in climbing can be eliminated, even by the most seasoned individuals.

The accidents that could have been prevented, and can therefore be learned from, include; solo climbing, climbing in poor conditions, using inadequate belay and rappel stations, and using poor judgment in route selection based on unfavorable conditions or ability.

There was a marked increase in the number of rescues that were initiated by cellular phone calls this year. It is unclear if this was due to improved cell phone reception or to an increase in the number of climbers taking phones with them on their climbs. Whatever the reason, use of cell phones generally resulted in much faster rescue times.

We would like to express our gratitude to the following individuals who contributed to the Canadian section of this year's book: Marc Ledwidge, Lisa Paulson, Burke Duncan, Ron Harris, David Henderson, Sonia Woolford, Josh Briggs, Mike Haden, Doug Fulford, Joanne Hansen, Diana MacGibbon, Sarah Cassidy, Greg Heide, Val Fraser, Michel Bolduc, Jonathan Fischer, Murray Toft and Helen Sovdat. Thanks also to those who fortunately either had nothing to report or who provided information that was not included in this year's book.

United States: The number of fatalities for this year—24—is nearly equal to the average number of same for the past decade. The number of accidents reported—150—is ten higher than the average for this same time period. Whether this is bad news or not depends upon several factors. We can assume there has been an increase in the number of people climbing and climber days, but this is a difficult number to determine. One area from which we received many reports this year—18—was Mount Shasta, which brought the California total much higher than in previous years. The unfortunate thing about these reports, over half of which involved sliding down snow out of control, is that nearly all the individuals were new to climbing—and some did not even have appropriate climbing equipment. We'll be paying close attention to this area, as it is obviously attracting people to attempt ascents. Its access, like Mount Hood and Mount Washington, as well as "roadside attractions" like Joshua Tree, can mean that non-climbers become part of our data and narratives, perhaps leading cursory readers to the wrong conclusions about the levels of risk and danger in the sport.

A continuing issue is the value of wearing a helmet while climbing. The basic purpose is to protect climbers from falling rocks and objects. In recent years, helmet designers have paid attention to side-impact in order to make helmets more useful in falls that result in head contact with the rock. Over the years, the number of rock climbing accidents in which climbers have had head impact on rock and are seriously or fatally injured is few. Most head impacts have occurred when the climber falls to the deck—and tumbles. In one of these cases this year (see the Mohonk Preserve report), a veteran climber assures us that a helmet saved his life—or at least his mental and physical functioning. On artificial climbing walls, helmets are not seen as a necessary item. To date, we have heard of no serious or fatal head injuries occurring on these venues.

There is certainly an increase in the number of incidents that occur when climbers use the "sling-shot" belay/lowering system. Misjudgements in rope length, how quickly speed can build up, weight ratios, and anchoring systems abound. From reading some of these mishaps, I am reminded of perfectly intelligent people trying to stuff a two-foot by three-foot bag into the overhead compartment on an airplane. Defies all logic.

Again we had some areas not reporting in this year, including Maine, Eldorado Canyon, and Smith Rock. Some individual reports came forward from these locations, but we could use help! A paragraph summary of New Hampshire accidents didn't provide enough detail for data or narratives.

In addition to the Safety Committee, we are grateful to the following—with apologies for any omissions—for collecting data and helping with the report: Hank Alicandri, Micki Canfield, Ron Cloud, Jim Detterline, Mark Magnuson, Bill May, Leo Paik, Robert Speik, all individuals who sent in personal stories, and, of course, George Sainsbury.

John E. (Jed) Williamson
Managing Editor
7 River Ridge Road
Hanover, NH 03755
e-mail: jedwmsn@sover.net

Nancy Hansen
Canadian Editor
Box 8040
Canmore, Alberta T1W 2T8
e-mail: nhansen@telusplanet.net

CANADA

FALLING ICE, POOR POSITION
Alberta, Banff National Park, Louise Falls

On January 20, a number of parties were climbing on this popular multi-pitch water ice Grade 4+ climb near Lake Louise. One of the parties high on the route dislodged a large piece of ice which hit S.G. He sustained crushing injuries to his left foot. He was able to rappel, but unable to walk back to the trailhead. He was evacuated by snowmobile by the Park Warden Service.

Analysis

As ice climbing continues to grow in popularity, certain routes are becoming more crowded and this type of accident is becoming more common. Parties should take note of their position in relation to others above them. Choosing a different line or abandoning the climb may be the most appropriate actions. (Source: Parks Canada Warden Service)

FALL ON ICE, PROTECTION FAILURE—ICE AX TOOL
Alberta, Banff National Park, Wicked Wanda

F.B. (32) was leading the crux pitch of this water ice Grade 4+ route on February 2. He was about three meters above an ice mushroom around which he had tied a sling. His ice tool unexpectedly popped out of the ice, causing a large piece of ice to fall on the ice mushroom with the sling, breaking the mushroom off. The screw he had placed six meters below the ice mushroom held his fall. Although this was in a relatively remote area, another climber was able to call for help on his cell phone. Because of gusty winds, the Warden Service rescue crew could only be inserted below the victim by heli-sling. The crew walked up to the site and the victim was lowered and carried down to a suitable landing area. He was then evacuated to the Banff Hospital. F.B. sustained injuries to his ankle and elbow and facial lacerations.

Analysis

Ice tool placement can be unreliable at times. It is unclear if the slung mushroom would have held his fall if the large piece of ice had not broken it off. (Source: Parks Canada Warden Service)

FALL ON ICE, CLIMBING ON THIN ICE
Alberta, Ghost River, The Sorcerer

On February 13, C.W. (26) and I, M.H. (38), were climbing The Sorcerer, a Grade V water ice climb. The first pitch went up a thin, mid-angled shield to a lower-angled dish from which the line headed right across slabby terrain and up to a short, steep wall. The ice was in thin condition, but no thinner than other climbing we had done earlier in the season. We discussed and analyzed the condition of the ice prior to beginning and both of us felt that it could be done safely with good protection available in between thin sections.

C.W. led the first pitch and placed three good ice screws in thick ice prior to reaching the short steep step with thin ice. I could no longer see him and after a noticeable pause I asked him how things were. He responded that he was somewhat unsure about the quality of the ice on the step and was considering retreating. Moments later I heard him yell and fall. The top ice screw held his fall of approximately seven to ten meters.

I was able to lower him directly down to the snow at the base of the climb. Our immediate diagnosis was a broken ankle. We reached 911 on his cell phone and a helicopter evacuation was arranged with Natural Resource Services, Kananaskis Country.

At the time of the fall, C.W. was standing on firm ground at the top of the slabs with his tools in the thin ice on the short steep wall. He was analyzing how well the ice was connected to the rock when he moved one tool slightly and felt the ice sheet give way. He fell feet-first, striking the lower angled slabs with his full weight on one cramponed foot. He was later diagnosed with a broken ankle and broken talus bone. He has had to give up climbing and will one day have to have the bones fused.

Analysis

What to learn from it? Some might say that there was a judgment error for us to consider climbing when the ice was so thin. Others would say that our analysis was sound and that we understood the risks of climbing thin ice and the potential costs of climbing such a pitch. I don't personally feel our judgment or experience were at fault. We simply chose to play the game and lost on the roll of a die. The most obvious lesson to learn from this is to have a heightened caution and attention when climbing through the transition from lower-angled terrain to steeper terrain. If the lower-angled slab had not been immediately beneath him, and he had fallen on steeper ground with nothing to hit, chances are he would be out climbing with me this weekend.

The practice of clipping one of the two ropes into each ice screw has become standard practice for many climbers. The idea is to create a larger "bungie" effect with the dynamic lines, reducing the force on the ice placement with the heightened risk of a slightly longer fall. Whether or not this was a contributing factor is unknown.

Without the cell phone, the management of the accident would have been much more difficult and time-consuming with perhaps very bad results. The blood flow in C.W.'s foot was severely reduced because of the angle of the ankle and the swelling. If he had been forced to stay out longer, there is a good chance that he could have lost the foot entirely. (Source: M.H.)

FALL ON SNOW, AVALANCHE (TWICE), POOR POSITION, LATE START, INADEQUATE EQUIPMENT—STOVE
Alberta, Lake Louise, Wapta Ice Field, Peyto Glacier Approach

On March 19, Ken Fischer (32), myself—Jonathan Fischer (29), and my wife Carey (31) began what we thought was to be a five day ski traverse of the Wapta Icefield. Due to logistical problems, we had gotten a late start and had started skiing at the embarrassingly late hour of noon. The route traverses Peyto Lake and then continues up a moraine to gain the Peyto Glacier. Our goal was to reach the Peyto Hut at the top of Peyto Glacier, a six-mile day.

While climbing up the moraine, we came to a decision point. Well marked cairns that we had been following traversed the upper east slope of the moraine, or an alternative route continued to the top of the moraine. It was late, nearly five o'clock, as we were making very slow progress because of heavy first-day packs and route finding problems at the base of the moraine. Ken decided to scout the cairned route as it looked promising and the cairns seemed logical up to that point. I said to Carey, "It's getting late and we're all tired; we're going to make a mistake and someone is going to get hurt." Seconds later, Ken radioed to me that he had slid out onto a steep snow slope and may need assistance. I hurried around the corner to find that Ken had slid about 30 feet out and down a small snow slope sandwiched between two rock outcroppings. The majority of the slope was windswept with lots of exposed rock. Ken had tried unsuccessfully to climb straight up the slope but encountered very deep snow conditions. He had our only rope. We decided the best thing to do would be to cut straight across the snow to the rock outcropping on which I was standing, maybe 20 feet away. He took one step in that direction when the slope avalanched, the fracture line occurring some 50 feet above him. He was swept over a rock face and out of sight. I screamed to Carey to grab our avalanche probes and shovels and scrambled down to the top of the rock face. My heart sank. The face dropped steeply for several hundred vertical feet. The chances of him surviving such a fall seemed low.

Carey then arrived with the shovels and avalanche probes. We dialed our avalanche beacons to "receive" and descended a short distance to a better vantage point where we could make out two objects at the base of the slope. After looking carefully for several seconds in the late afternoon shade, we concluded that one was Ken and the other his backpack. There was no sign of movement and we could not tell if he was lying face up or down.

We considered our options. Going up or across the moraine to obtain easier ground to the bottom of the valley would expose us to additional avalanche paths and would be very time consuming. We concluded that we must descend the slope if we were to have any chance of helping Ken. The temperature was now in the single digits and he would not survive long partially buried in the snow, assuming that he was still alive. Carey went back up to retrieve our gear, as we would need it to set up camp on the valley bottom. I began the descent. The climbing was mostly 4th class with occasional stretches of lower 5th class, but seemed much harder under these conditions. I found Ken lying with his head downhill and face up. He was conscious, but very disoriented and had signs of being hypothermic. He had lost his hat and gloves in the fall and his jacket had filled up with snow. His face was badly bloodied and he was missing one of his front teeth. He had complete movement in his arms and legs and no pain in his lower back or neck. A spinal injury, at least, seemed unlikely. He sat up on his own and complained about severe pain in his lower left rib cage. I put as much clothing on him as I could and put him on a mat with his sleeping bag around him. I radioed to Carey that Ken was alive. She suggested that she throw down our backpacks, as negotiating the steep slope with a heavy pack was out of the question. Carey pushed the packs over the rock face. Watching them pinball down the slope a vertical distance of 400 to 450 feet made me think what a miracle it was that Ken had survived such a fall. Carey then strapped the skis together and pushed them down the slope, but they got caught up at a very precarious point on the rock face. "We'll worry about them later," I radioed to Carey.

I positioned myself at a point where I could see the entire descent and radioed to Carey what I thought would be the best route. She was making good progress when she was slowed by the most difficult climbing slightly more than half way down the slope. I started to get concerned about her ability to negotiate the 5th class rock. I grabbed the rope from Ken's pack and began to ascend. I realized that the rope's usefulness would be limited, because anchor possibilities were few. I gained a bench maybe 30 feet below her. I could see my footsteps on a small strip of snow that traversed upwards connecting the two of us. Carey was on a small patch of snow maybe five feet from where my footsteps were. There was absolutely no way that I thought that the tiny patch of snow on which she stood could possibly avalanche, particularly considering that I had cut across the corner of the snow patch maybe five feet away. I was wrong. A fracture line ripped across the snow patch approximately 15 feet above Carey, sending her tumbling out of control. The bench I was standing on was several feet wide and I felt secure. In the heat of the moment, I naively thought that I could traverse the bench and stop her descent, as the volume of snow falling seemed relatively small. I ran across the bench to intersect her fall line, only to find the bench faded to exposed rock. I realized my mistake and tried to retreat, but it was too late. What seemed like a trivial amount of snow on the outer edges of the avalanche hit me with an unbelievable amount of force, peeling me off the rock and tumbling me down the steep slope. I smashed my face and then slammed hard on my right side on a bench 100 feet below. My momentum, however, carried me off the bench and down another 25 feet where I landed feet first on a large pile of snow. After several seconds of disorientation, I screamed for Carey who quickly appeared on the bench 25 feet above me. She scrambled around and down to where I was. My face was bloodied and I had injured my wrist, but it was still functional. Carey had hit the side of her head and broken her glasses as well as severely bruised her legs. We had both fallen approximately 125 vertical feet, but managed to avoid serious injury.

We descended easy ground to reach Ken and found that his condition had worsened. We needed to get him in a tent quickly, out of the wind. Our position was threatened by dangerous hang-fire some 500 feet above us. Considering the avalanche conditions, the winter environment, and the distance to the trailhead, we decided it would be dangerous for Carey or me to try and go for help at night. Every conceivable place to set up a tent seemed scree covered or in an avalanche path, so we settled on an awkward spot in the scree. Carey set up the tent while I tried to start the stove. (We had just purchased a new stove the night before, as the airlines had confiscated our trusty stove, even though it did not have any fuel in it.) For the life of me, I could not get the stove to start. We both knew that we would pass a difficult night without the stove, trying to keep Ken from reaching a profound hypothermic state. It was a miserable night with temperatures dropping to -10 degrees F with a moderate wind, but we survived.

I got up before dawn to scout a route out. I had intended on going for help, as I doubted Ken's ability to walk out on his own. I traveled down the valley several hundred yards to a corniced 40-foot drop that had stopped our progress along the valley bottom the day before. If we could get down that, we would be on familiar ground for 3.5 miles to the trailhead. I went back to camp to find that Ken was up and moving and wanted to hike out. I attempted to retrieve the skis while Carey packed up, but was unsuccessful. The terrain was simply too technical and I was, logically, very concerned about additional avalanches. I retreated, discouraged, knowing that it was going to be long hike out without our skis. Ken's skis were apparently buried in the avalanche, as there was no sign of them.

I returned to camp and we began our hike out. We rappelled down the steep corniced part, which had surprisingly stable snow conditions. After several hours of exhausting post-holing, we reached the car and took Ken to the hospital in Canmore where he was diagnosed with three broken ribs, a pneumothorax, a missing tooth, a severe cut on his elbow, chipped ulna, and several severe lacerations on his face that required stitches. He was admitted to the hospital for treatment of the pneumothorax.

Four days later, on his 33rd birthday, Ken was about to be discharged from the hospital. However, only minutes before his release, he collapsed and was paralyzed on his right side and was unable to speak. The doctors suspected a stroke, and he was transferred via ambulance to a regional stroke center in Calgary for specialized treatment. In Calgary it was diagnosed that a massive clot had blocked the main artery to the left side of his brain. A special blood thinning drug, t-PA, was administered through a catheter directly into the clot, saving his life. Although it was never determined definitively, the doctors suspected that the stroke may have been caused by a clot formed in the carotid artery which could have been damaged in the fall. He was released from the hospital a week later and has been undergoing stroke rehabilitation with tremendous success.

Analysis

The late start from the trailhead contributed to this accident. The snow was more unstable in the late afternoon, and we were moving anxiously, and therefore not as safely, fighting daylight to reach the hut. The terrain that Ken was on was not an obvious avalanche path from our perspective. The presence of exposed rocks giving it a sense of security, but obviously not preventing it from avalanching.

Having a dysfunctional stove when it was really needed shows the importance of inspecting and testing all gear prior to a trip.

Given the mechanism of injury, we should have been more concerned about a potential spinal injury than we were. We let ourselves get distracted by his painful rib injury and the urgency to treat the hypothermia.

I believe the fact that we had been prepared to camp out and had carried a tent, even though we had been planning on staying in huts throughout the trip, may have saved Ken's life. Had a storm decided to hit that night, it most certainly would have saved us all. Considering the always present difficulties of route finding in winter conditions and the possibility that an injury or equipment problem could quite easily cause one not to reach the hut, it seems foolish to not be prepared for an unplanned bivouac on such trips. (Source: Jonathan Fischer) *(Editor's Note: Thanks to Jonathan Fischer for sending this thorough account and analysis.)*

FALL ON ROCK—NO BELAY, LACK OF COMMUNICATION
Alberta, Banff National Park, Back of the Lake
On June 17, two experienced sport climbers were climbing a 25-meter, 5.11a route called Mardi Gras. G.H. (36) had just finished the route on a top rope, and yelled down, "Okay," thinking that he was going to be lowered by the belayer, T.G. (35). The belayer yelled up, "Okay," and removed the rope from her belay device, thinking that G.H. was going to rappel. G.H. paused to straighten the rope, then let go of the anchor chain and leaned back. G.H. free-fell for approximately 19 meters before T.G. grabbed the rope and managed to stop the fall with her bare hands. She was quickly assisted by neighboring climbers and later treated for severe rope burns to both hands.
Analysis
This incident shows the reason for the development of standard climbing signals. It is extremely important for climbers not to become too casual with their communication. (Source: G.H., Nancy Hansen)

SLIP ON MIXED TERRAIN, INADEQUATE EQUIPMENT (ICE AX IN PACK), EXCEEDING ABILITIES
Alberta, Banff National Park, Cascade Mountain
The story behind this accident was largely pieced together from the evidence gathered during the lengthy search that was required to locate and recover the victim's body. The victim, P.O. (19), planned on climbing the south face of Cascade Mountain with two friends. P.O.'s day off work (June 23) arrived a day before the other two were available, so he told one of the others he would head up the lower part of the mountain alone to reconnoiter the route which they would try the next day together. When he failed to return that night, his friends notified Warden Service dispatch and a search commenced. His body was finally located on July 7.
Analysis
The south face of Cascade Mountain is 1200 meters high and consists mostly of steep scree gullies and rock slabs. In June of 2000, snow still covered about two-thirds of the route due to an unseasonably cold spring.

It was determined that P.O., using crampons and an ice ax, kicked steps in snow gullies well up the face. When he reached dry rock and open scree, he removed and packed his crampons and ice ax. Several hundred meters higher he was forced to traverse left across a wide snow bowl at the head of the main gully system. Apparently, to avoid the need to stop and get the crampons and ice ax out of his pack, he tried to follow a narrow, down-sloping ledge of dry rock. When he slipped and fell off, he landed on the hard snow below. Without his ice ax he was unable to self-arrest. He fell about 300 meters down the main gully, then slipped into a small moat and was covered by snow that had dislodged during his fall. He died of multiple trauma.

P.O. came to western Canada to climb. He had trained in the east and had obtained the proper equipment. The late spring conditions were likely frustrating to him, as they were to many. The south face of Cascade Mountain is one of the closest mountain climbs to downtown Banff. It is not the usual route to the top, but the angle is mostly moderate, so when P.O. found the step-kicking straightforward, his reconnaissance must have turned into an irresistible urge to bag his first Rockies summit. (Source: Parks Canada Warden Service)

FALL ON ROCK, CARABINER FAILURE—PROBABLY CROSS-LOADED
Alberta, Banff National Park, Back of the Lake

On July 29, A.L. was attempting to redpoint "Howard the Duck", a 5.11a sport rock climb at the Lake Louise crags. He had clipped the first two bolts and placed a quick-draw on the third just below the crux. He felt unable to clip his rope into the third quick-draw and began to down-climb to minimize the distance he might fall. When his weight came onto the second quick-draw following his fall, the carabiner clipped into the bolt hanger failed. A.L. fell to the ground. Unfortunately, there was a log where he landed and he was impaled in the back by a branch of about ten centimeters thick and 15 centimeters long. The accident was reported almost immediately to Warden Service dispatch by cell phone. A.L. was evacuated by helicopter to the Banff Hospital by Warden Service rescue crews.

Analysis

It is speculated that the carabiner clipped to the bolt hanger flipped and became cross-loaded while A.L. was working on the difficult, overhanging moves. The carabiner was still in one piece with the gate attached at the hinge but the other end was blown open and had come off the hanger.

The victim was extremely lucky that the branch did not penetrate any vital organs. It entered his back behind his heart and became lodged between his shoulder blade and ribcage. (Source: Parks Canada Warden Service)

HANDHOLD CAME OFF—FALL ON ROCK, PROTECTION (BOLT) PULLED OUT
Alberta, Lady MacDonald, Stoneworks Crag

On August 4, S. (20) was climbing a 5.12a sport route at a crag near Canmore. He clipped three bolts and moved some distance above the third bolt when a hold pulled off the rock and he fell. The top bolt ripped out, causing him to fall six meters to the ground. He shattered the bones in one foot and fractured the other, requiring eight hours of surgery. He was heli-slung to the Canmore Hospital. (Source: Natural Resources Service, Kananaskis Country)

Analysis

S. said that the bolt looked good when he clipped it, and suspects that the rock surrounding the bolt may have failed. Climbers should be cognizant of the fact that poor rock or poorly placed or old bolts can be prone to pulling out or breaking. However, considering the number of bolts that are clipped every year by sport climbers in North America, this type of incident is relatively rare. (Source: Nancy Hansen)

FALLING ROCK–DISLODGED, FALL ON SNOW, NO BELAY OR PROTECTION
Alberta, Banff National Park, Mount Lefroy

On August 18, four climbers were ascending the 45-degree snow-and-ice route on Mount Lefroy. They were traveling as two independent rope teams, moving together with short lengths of rope between the climbers. At 3400 meters, the route narrows into a gully bordered by rock. One of the lead climbers dislodged a rock which struck the lower climber, causing both members of the team to lose their balance and fall about 300 meters down the route. The other two climbers climbed down to assess and stabilize them. One climber descended to the Abbot Pass Hut to use the emergency phone. Upon discovering that the phone was not working, he began heading further down the mountain for help when he ran into another climber with a cell phone. Both climbers were evacuated via heli-sling by Warden Service rescue crews. They had sustained multiple fractures, bruising, and puncture wounds from crampons.
Analysis
It is common practice for climbers to travel together with a short length of rope between them on straightforward terrain. Part of the challenge and risk in mountaineering includes assessing when the terrain and conditions dictate setting up anchors and pitching out the route. (Source: Parks Canada Warden Service)

FALLING ROCK
Alberta, Banff National Park, Mount Little

On August 29, a party of four was ascending the normal route on Mount Little during an Association of Canadian Mountain Guides Assistant Alpine Guide exam. Two candidates were roped together and a third was roped to the examiner. As they were walking along the base of the ridge a large rock fell from the ridge crest about ten meters above them and struck the examiner on the head. The other climbers attempted resuscitation, but it appeared that the victim had died instantly. They attempted to call Park Dispatch by radio, but the radio was not functioning. Two of the climbers descended to Moraine Lake to report the accident. One stayed with the victim and continued resuscitation attempts. He had a cell phone with which he was eventually able to get a connection through to Warden Service dispatch. At this point, it was snowing heavily and the rescue helicopter was only able to land on the toe of the upper glacier. Warden Service rescue crews climbed to the scene and confirmed the fatality. The weather deteriorated further and the helicopter was unable to fly down. The guide candidate descended to Moraine Lake and the pilot and two rescuers spent the night with the helicopter. By mid-morning the next day, the weather improved enough to allow the helicopter to complete the evacuation of the rescuers and the body.

Analysis

All of the climbers were wearing helmets. This is a heavily traveled route, possibly the most popular in the Ten Peaks area. This section of the climb was not known for rockfall. There were no smaller rocks or debris which accompanied the large block and which may have provided some warning. This incident is a reminder that there are inherent risks in mountaineering that cannot be completely eliminated. (Source: Parks Canada Warden Service, Helen Sovdat)

FALL ON ICE/SNOW, UNROPED, POOR ROUTE CHOICE, HASTE
Alberta, Columbia Icefield, Mount Athabasca

On August 29 at 0500, F.W. (43), S.C. (34), and U.T. (37) set out to climb the North Face of Mount Athabasca. They reached the summit at 1730 and started to descend by the normal route. The group found that their crampons were balling up with the wet snow, but a hard layer ten centimeters down made them decide to keep their crampons on. At the top of a snow-and-ice feature known as the Silverhorn, F.W. began to descend the steep snow slope instead of taking the easier shale trail to the left. S.C. suggested they follow the shale trail down, but F.W. felt that it would be quicker to go down the snow slope. F.W. started down the slope and then turned to face in, saying that it was getting icy. S.C. was about ten meters above F.W. and heard him shout and watched him fall down the steep slope and out of sight. F.W. did not respond when S.C. and U.T. called him. They descended the shale trail and short-roped down the standard route. Near the base of the Silverhorn, they saw F.W.'s ice ax above the bergschrund, 400 meters below where he had slipped.

At 1900, S.C. climbed to the bergschrund edge and found F.W. one meter down and lying on secure snow. He responded to his name but had obviously sustained multiple injuries. S.C. left F.W. lying on his side and put extra clothing around him to keep him warm and stabilize his neck. U.T. was a less experienced mountaineer, and S.C. did not want to leave U.T. with the victim in the worsening weather, nor allow U.T. to go down the crevassed glacier by herself. So S.C. descended with U.T. to get help.

At the toe of the glacier, they met two other climbers. D.R. went back up to the bergschrund and reached F.W. at 2030, while S.C. descended to get help from the Warden Service. F.W. was unresponsive and his airway was blocked with blood. D.R. did CPR for an hour with no response or signs of life and so left F.W. to hike down. D.R. met up with responding Park Wardens and a Medic on the moraine near the base of the mountain. With D.R.'s news, it was decided to wait until morning to recover F.W.'s body.

Heavy snowfall that night prevented the Park Wardens from flying to the site until 1100 the following day, at which time they did avalanche control with explosives to make the site safe for rescuers. Two size 1.5-2.0 slab avalanches released and buried F.W. with two meters of snow. At 1325, his body was heli-slung off Mount Athabasca.

Analysis

F.W. was an experienced mountaineer and a member of a search and rescue team in New Zealand. The group was in a hurry to descend after spending longer on the ascent than they had expected. It is likely that F.W.'s slip was caused by his crampons balling up with wet snow on the initial, lower angled part of his chosen descent route. The hard snow and ice surface on the steep face that followed prevented him from self-arresting his fall. After recognizing the poor snow conditions on the summit ridge, F.W. could have opted for the safer route down the shale trail, or could have asked for a roped belay to check out the snow descent. (Source: Lisa Paulson, Jasper National Park Warden Service, S.C., member of climbing party)

HANDHOLD CAME OFF—FAILURE TO TEST HOLD, FALL ON ROCK, CLIMBING UNROPED
Alberta, Jasper National Park, Mount Colin

On September 7, S.A. (35) and L.B. (26) set out to climb Mount Colin by the Southwest Face Direct route (III 5.7). The pair decided to solo the first few 5.5 pitches to save time. At 0900, one hour into the climb, S.A. was thrown out of balance when he grabbed a loose handhold. He fell 60 to 80 meters. L.B. saw him unsuccessfully try to stand up.

Park Wardens heli-slung into the area and climbed to the victim. S.A. had come to rest on a ledge in a steep rock gully to the left of the buttress he was climbing. S.A. had died from extensive trauma. His body was lowered off the mountain and heli-slung down to the awaiting ambulance.

Analysis

Climbers are sometimes lured into solo climbing easier pitches. However, Canadian Rockies limestone is often loose, particularly on lower-angled terrain, which is why it is a good idea to rope up. (Source: Lisa Paulson, Jasper National Park Warden Service)

AVALANCHE, FALL ON SNOW, INADEQUATE PROTECTION
Alberta, Jasper National Park, Mount Woolley

On November 13 at 1000, a party of three (ages: 25, 26, 26) set out to climb the Japanese Couloir of Mount Woolley on a clear morning with light winds. They were climbing together, equally spaced along a 50 meter by nine millimeter rope with one ice screw in between each climber. The climb was mostly hard snow and ice on a slope angle ranging between 40 and 50 degrees. Around 1215, the lead climber was near the top of the couloir when the snow became boot-top deep and he triggered a slab avalanche up to 50 centimeters deep by about 50 meters wide. The lead climber was knocked off his feet and was swept down with the avalanche. One of the group members believes the rope broke when all three climbers momentarily hung from the highest screw. It is likely that the second screw pulled out when it was shock loaded. All three climbers fell approximately 500 meters over hard snow, ice, and rock outcrops.

When the avalanche came to rest, one climber was on the surface, the second was buried to his neck, and the third climber's legs were buried. The distance between the climbers suggested that the rope did indeed break.

The entire incident was observed by J.B. (23), who was staying at the Mount Alberta hut at the base of the Japanese Couloir. He grabbed sleeping bags, sleeping pads and a shovel from the hut and ran 15 minutes to the fallen climbers. J.B. dug them out, cut off their harnesses and packs where necessary, wrapped them in sleeping bags, placed them on sleeping pads, replaced their helmets with toques, and left them with food, water, and a guide's tarp. J.B. left the scene at 1300 and was at the highway by 1500 (normally a five to six hour trip). He asked a passing motorist to call 911 while he drove to the Sunwapta Warden Station.

At 1617, a helicopter from Golden arrived at the staging area and took three Wardens and one Paramedic to the scene. The residual avalanche hazard was evaluated and found to be nonthreatening. Time was the main concern as there was limited daylight left to evacuate the victims. At 1638, rescuers arrived on scene and the patients were assessed. Climber 1 had a fractured pelvis, concussion, and fractured vertebrate. Climber 2 had a hemothorax. Climber 3 had a fractured pelvis and punctured bladder. By 1726, all victims and rescuers were evacuated.

Analysis

Prior to leaving, the party spoke with a Public Safety Warden, who advised them that in the past week, approximately 30 centimeters of snow had fallen with moderate southwest winds in the area. An avalanche bulletin posted on November 8 indicated there was moderate hazard in the alpine and advised that soft slabs may exist on wind-loaded slopes. The party consisted of experienced climbers who admittedly were driven with the anticipation of the views ahead on the nearby summit. Had the party looked more closely at the shallow gully above which was lined with a lateral cornice on the left, they may have detected the slab earlier. Earlier detection may have given them the option to turn around or possibly to choose to go up and right to a rib of scree and shallow snow.

Simultaneous climbing with protection placement is a climbing style used to move quickly when travel is good, the chances of a fall are minimal, and the consequences are not serious. In this case, if only one climber had gone on to assess the snow while the other two were anchored off to the side at a belay, the risk may have been minimized. Whether or not a thicker rope would have made a difference in this situation is unknown, as it may have been the screws that failed under the weight of the three climbers. The rope was buried under the avalanche debris, so the exact cause of the equipment failure remains a mystery. (Source: Lisa Paulson, Jasper National Park Warden Service, J.B., rescuer)

RAPPEL FAILURE—MISPERCEPTION OF ANCHOR, FALL ON ICE
Alberta, Banff National Park, Selenium Falls

On December 12, a party of three had completed Selenium Falls, a water ice Grade 5 route. To descend, the climbers threaded their ropes through an existing Abalokov (V-thread) in the ice. A V-thread anchor is created by threading and unthreading two ice screws at an angle to one another through the ice and then threading a cord through the channel. A knot is tied on the outside to create a hanging loop. In this case, the cord had iced over since its original installation and the climbers mistook the long tail end of the cord for the main, knotted part of the loop. When the first climber, D.J. (40) began to rappel, the loose tail pulled out of the ice and he fell 140 meters to the base of the climb, sustaining fatal injuries. The other two climbers hiked up to the ridge and traversed over to the gondola station at the summit of the mountain. Two hours after the fall, they were able to alert Warden Service dispatch. By then it was dark, but Warden Service rescue crews climbed up to the route prepared to do a stretcher evacuation. The climber was located at the base of the route. His body was evacuated the next morning by heli-sling.

Analysis
V-thread anchors are a common and reliable method for setting up rappels on waterfall ice. However, they should always be backed up with an ice screw anchor until the last climber descends. This is particularly important when using previously installed anchors. (Source: Parks Canada Warden Service)

FALL ON ICE, CLIMBING ALONE AND UNROPED
Alberta, Roche a Perdix, Drambuie Deamon
On December 16, I.R. attempted to solo climb Drambuie Deamon, a 95-meter water ice Grade 3 or 4 route, depending on the chosen finish for the climb. He had been climbing for two years and had done the climb before. I.R. dropped his wife off in Hinton at 1200 and planned to pick her up by 1500. His wife called for assistance at 1745 when I.R had not returned. Jasper National Park Wardens responded that night. I.R. was found dead near the base of the climb with ice tools attached to his wrists and his rope coiled and on his pack.

Analysis
It is difficult to conclude exactly what caused I.R. to fall, but ice quality was likely poor, as the week prior had been very cold with minimum temperatures of –30 degrees C. (Source: Lisa Paulson, Jasper National Park Warden Service)

AVALANCHE, FALL ON SNOW AND ROCK, POOR POSITION—UNSAFE CONDITIONS
British Columbia, Yoho National Park, Mount Burgess
On April 21, a party of two had ascended the south-facing, avalanche-prone slopes of Mount Burgess. The day was very warm, resulting in one of the first major isothermal avalanche cycles of the spring. The party was descending about ten minutes apart. When M.K. reached the first avalanche slope they had traversed while ascending, he saw that the slope had avalanched and realized that J.M. had been carried over the large cliff below. He retraced their ascent route but was unable to find his partner. He then returned to the highway to report the accident. The Park Warden Service was contacted just before dark at 2030. Due to the high avalanche risk, it was not possible to search

the area by ground that evening. An air search was begun at first light. J.M. was located on top of the debris from a large second avalanche. He had been carried over a large cliff by the first slide which triggered the second avalanche. He was unconscious and barely alive when Park Warden rescuers reached him. He was severely hypothermic (his core temperature was measured at 25 degrees C later that day), and he had suffered an almost complete amputation of one lower leg. The victim was stabilized, flown to the Banff Hospital with the rescue helicopter and transferred to a Calgary hospital by air ambulance. He had fallen a distance of 300 meters. He later recalled being partially buried in the second avalanche and digging his way out with his ice ax. He recalls trying to stay awake, but eventually lost consciousness.

Analysis

It was an extremely warm day with many large spring avalanches running. The party had underestimated the avalanche risk and were on the slopes too late in the day. It is speculated that when the victim hit the lower avalanche slope after being carried over the 300-meter-high cliff face, the ensuing avalanche may have provided a cushioning effect which likely contributed to his survival. There is also speculation that the hypothermia may have reduced the amount of bleeding from his severely injured leg. (Source: Parks Canada Warden Service)

FALL ON ROCK, INADEQUATE PROTECTION—BELAY ANCHOR, INADEQUATE BELAY
British Columbia, Squamish, Sickle

Two climbers were ascending a route called Sickle on the Apron on May 20. They were anchored to a conifer tree, about five to ten centimeters in diameter and three meters tall. The lead climber fell, pulling off the belayer and the tree. They fell about 40 meters and were caught by a clump of trees. One suffered a broken ankle and ribs, and both were bruised and cut. (Source: CASBC Access News #21)

Analysis

Trees on steep cliffs are often poorly rooted. Climbers should always examine the tree carefully, test it, and back it up with more protection if there is any doubt. (Source: Nancy Hansen)

SLIP ON MIXED TERRAIN, RAPPEL ERROR, FATIGUE, DEHYDRATION
British Columbia, Tantalus Range, Mount Dione

On September 24, two experienced climbers were descending Mount Dione. They had completed the second ascent of the West Face, and spent the night on the summit. H.Z. (39) had forgotten his water bottle and was very dehydrated. Both climbers were fatigued and were rappelling and down-climbing the standard descent route. The final rappel was over steep rock and snow. M.S. rappelled from an anchor made of natural rock protection. H.Z. told M.S. that he would remove the rock gear and either make a bollard in the snow to rappel from or down-climb. Somewhere between moving the rappel anchor or beginning the down-climb, H.Z. slipped and fell 30 meters. He sustained a fractured pelvis and internal injuries, and then went into cardiac arrest. He was heli-evacuated by the Squamish and Whistler Search and Rescue teams. He died three days later in hospital, never having regained consciousness.

Analysis:

H.Z. was severely dehydrated and fatigued, and it is likely that his judgment and movement on the terrain were impaired as a result. (Source: Val Fraser, Squamish Search & Rescue)

ROCK HOLDING PROTECTION BROKE OFF—FALL ON ROCK, PROTECTION PULLED OUT
British Columbia, Yoho National Park, Mount Stephen

On September 27, a party of three were attempting a new route on the China Wall of Mount Stephen. They had ascended the lower 300 meters of fifth class climbing on the route and were beginning the 500 meters of overhanging aid climbing. D.E. was leading an A3 pitch and was drilling a ⁵⁄₁₆-inch rivet while hanging on a hook. Just after placing the hanger on the rivet, the rock broke under his hook and he fell about 20 meters, pulling out two removable bolts. He was finally caught by a ⁵⁄₁₆-inch rivet. He sustained deep lacerations to his knee in the fall. The party contacted Warden Service dispatch by radio and rescue crews were overflying the scene shortly afterwards. With some extremely skillful flying, the rescue pilot with Alpine Helicopters was able to sling a rescuer into the scene and evacuate the injured climber. (Source: Parks Canada Warden Service)

Analysis

The climbers were using advanced and appropriate aid technique. Hooking and placing rivets are methods used sparingly by aid climbers to get them through stretches with few other options for protection. As rivets generally only hold body weight, D.E. was lucky that one stopped his long fall. (Source: Murray Toft)

(Editor's note: There were several other climbing accidents which resulted in injury in British Columbia during 2000. We were unable to obtain sufficient data on these accidents to report them).

FALL ON ROCK, INADEQUATE PROTECTION, EXCEEDING ABILITIES
Ontario, Milton, Buffalo Crag

On Sunday, April 2, G.S. (56) was leading Tapestry, a one-pitch 5.8 rock climb. He placed good protection just before setting outwards over a small roof to tackle a thin crack on a bulge. He got several meters higher when his arms "burned out." As the face was overhanging, he opted for a controlled fall. He jumped outwards a little, fell straight down an estimated nine meters, halted for an instant as the rope stopped stretching, then swung violently back into the face, striking it with his right foot. Both bones in the lower leg shattered and pierced the skin. He was lowered by his partner, who then called 911 on a cell phone. The Milton Fire Department evacuated G.S. to the local hospital, which transferred him to the regional trauma center in nearby Hamilton. There, x-rays revealed four fractures in the foot along with the broken tibia and fibula. Before he was wheeled into surgery he was warned that amputation was a possibility. However, surgeons were able to save the leg by installing four plates during the five-and-a-half hour operation.

Analysis

G.S. had been climbing for six years and was an experienced leader in mid-level routes. He says he had been pushing it that day as he was not in top form, but did not feel he had been reckless. He says he never imagined how quickly the forces build up in a pendulum type of fall. He compared the impact to that of jumping off a three-story building to a concrete sidewalk.

There is a tree growing out of the bulge, but the route description in the guidebook admonishes using it for the sake of climbing style—climbers may be wise to ignore this. Had G.S. slung the tree for protection he could have reduced his fall to a meter or two. G.S. was wearing silk long underwear and it kept dirt from entering the ugly wounds and open bones and may have saved his leg from amputation. Interviewed for this report, G.S. asked that it be impressed upon readers the long-lasting consequences of a simple fall. Doctors originally indicated he would be active again in four to six months. However, the leg fractures reopened seven months later and further surgery was required, delaying G.S.'s recovery to an estimated two years in total.

G.S. also points out that the rescue operation took over three hours to get him to a hospital that is only ten minutes away. Any efforts that other climbers can make to get an injured climber to the cliff top, provided they don't endanger the injured climber, could cut hours off the rescue time. (Source: David Henderson)

FALL ON ICE, HARNESS CAME OFF—NOT BUCKLED CORRECTLY AND NOT CLIPPED IN TO LEG YOKES
Quebec, Gatineau Park, Cabin Creek Falls

On January 15, R.P. (48) began to climb Cabin Creek Falls, a water ice Grade 2 or 3 climb, depending on the line taken. He was belayed on top-rope by M.B. Both climbers had previous ice climbing experience. The rope was tied with a figure eight knot loop with a locking carabiner attached to it for the climber to clip into his/her harness. The climbers exchanged the standard information to indicate they were both ready and R.P. started up the route.

As R.P. started up the steeper section of the climb, his hand slipped out of his tool and he fell one or two feet, leaving his ice tool in place. M.B. helped R.P. reach his ice tool by applying all her weight to the rope to help "heave" him up. From there, R.P. climbed up and over the steep section and then asked to be lowered. R.P. began to lower over the steep part of the wall when he suddenly became airborne. He fell four meters, bounced on an ice ledge and then slid down another ten meters head first on his back. He was stopped by a large rock.

R.P. was unconscious for about two minutes. Other climbers called 911 and began an initial assessment of the victim. They were careful not to move him for fear of spinal injury. Warm clothing was placed around and over the victim.

The other climbers noticed that the waist belt of R.P.'s harness was not threaded through the buckle as it should have been.

Volunteer police and fire officials and the Emergency Medical Team arrived on the scene. Transportation of the litter down the hill took approximately one hour, with about 25 people involved. R.P. was diagnosed with a broken clavicle, four broken vertebrae, four broken ribs, a bruised lung, a fracture in the bone area under the eye, lacerations to the face and back of the head and undetermined head injuries. (Source: Diana MacGibbon, Ottawa)

Analysis

The top rope system was examined and found to be sound, including the presence of the still-locked carabiner attached to the figure eight knot at the climber's end of the rope. An inspection of R.P.'s harness revealed no obvious damage, and the climbers testing it after the accident found that they could not pull the waist belt apart even when it was only passed through the buckle once (i.e. not doubled back). It is possible that R.P. did "double back" the harness, but failed initially to pass the webbing through both sections of the buckle. The harness had a leg yoke separate from the waist belt and the two were intended to be connected by a carabiner. R.P. did not clip the locking carabiner through the leg yoke.

Many climbers are taught at an early stage to check their partner's harness before climbing. As climbers become more experienced, practices such as this are often discontinued. No matter what experience level, it is always a good idea to look at your partner's set up, particularly when bulky winter clothing may have obstructed their view of the harness.

Although it may not have affected the outcome of this accident, many climbers argue that top-roping with a carabiner attached to a figure eight knot is unacceptable because of the risk of a cross-loaded carabiner gate. It is safer practice to tie directly the rope directly into the harness. (Source: Diana MacGibbon, Ottawa; Nancy Hansen)

FALLING ROCK—HANDHOLD CAME OFF
Quebec, Gatineau Park, Home Cliff

On April 15, several climbers were top-roping on "Home Cliff" at the Luskville Escarpment. C.M. (33) had reached the top of his climb and was making his way above the other climbers over to one of the anchors. There is a low angled slab above the middle route where the anchors are located. C.M. was partway up the slab and was on a ledge, approximately six meters back from the edge of the cliff. He stepped down from the ledge onto the slab and felt something move under his feet. He then noticed a boulder, 45 centimeters in diameter, rolling towards the edge of the cliff about three meters away from him. He yelled "rock" to the climbers below. The rock landed on the left foot of one of the belayers.

A cell phone was used to call emergency services. Other climbers applied first aid to the victim, P.M. All of the climbers in the area assisted with P.M.'s evacuation, which involved moving him in a litter down steep terrain via a system of belays and fixed ropes. P.M suffered soft tissue damage and had to have one of his middle toes partly amputated. (Source: Diana MacGibbon, Ottawa)

Analysis

It is impossible to completely eliminate the risk of rock fall while climbing. In this case, it is lucky that nobody suffered greater injuries. (Source: Nancy Hansen)

FALLING ROCK, HANDHOLD FAILED
Quebec, Mont Gros Bras

S.C. (25) and R.B. (29) were climbing "Valerie Reverie", a 5.8 route at Mont Gros Bras. R.B. was leading the chimney on the third pitch when he pulled off a large rock which hit S.C. on the left side of his back. R.B. rappelled to the base of the route with S.C. and called for help on his cell phone. A helicopter from the Canadian Armed Forces was sent to evacuate the victim. S.C. suffered from four fractured ribs, perforated lungs, and a lumbar and cervical sprain.

Analysis

The rock is generally very loose on this mountain and so R.B. had been careful to test each hold. The block that pulled had appeared solid until it was fully weighted. Whenever possible climbers should attempt to place belay stations off to the side or under an overhang for protection from falling rock. (Source: Michel Bolduc, Quebec, and Nancy Hansen)

UNITED STATES

SLIP ON ICE, AMS, EXPOSURE, INADEQUATE CLOTHING, INEXPERIENCE
Alaska, Mount McKinley, West Buttress.

May 13, Rangers Kevin Moore and Scott Metcalfe with volunteers Jay Hammond and John Evans carried loads from 14,200 feet to 16,200 feet on the West Buttress and returned to 14,200 feet. They reported the following.

We saw Erik Seedhouse (35) and Doina Nugent (38) moving slowly at 15,300 feet just below the fixed lines on the headwall. They had moved maybe 400 feet in one and a half hours. We caught up to them and asked Nugent if they were feeling all right. He replied they were all right. Seedhouse had stopped continuously, and we thought he might be demonstrating symptoms of altitude sickness. We told them the symptoms of Acute Mountain Sickness and Seedhouse agreed he might have AMS. We suggested they go down and acclimatize slowly. But Nugent said sharply to Seedhouse that he didn't have AMS and that he was "a baby."

This interaction concerned me for a couple of reasons. First, Seedhouse did not want to climb, but Nugent was pushing him to continue. Nugent's expedition behavior did not show compassion for Seedhouse—who clearly was having difficulties. Second, Seedhouse was sunburnt, improperly dressed, and equipment was attached haphazardly to his pack, indicating he wasn't taking care of himself properly.

Nugent and Seedhouse sat down and we continued up the headwall to 16,200 feet where we spent the next three hours working. While descending the fixed lines, we received a radio call that a woman spent three hours stuck in the bergschrund, and might need assistance. We descended to the bergschrund and found Nugent and Seedhouse there. They were being assisted by the GT Expedition (Yvon Methot and Marc Talbot) and members of their own expedition.

Nugent had attached an ascender to the fixed line. The ascender became wedged between the rope and the icy lip of the bergschrund. Seedhouse and Nugent could not help themselves out of this jam. Methot and Talbot carried Nugent's pack and belayed them. At this point, we witnessed Seedhouse fall. Seedhouse slid about six feet and was caught by the rope. It took him a few moments and some effort to right himself, and when he did, he screamed, "My leg, my leg." Seedhouse shouted at Nugent, who was ignoring him, "I'll never forgive you for this! Never."

But Seedhouse was not injured and the group returned to 14,200 feet. Methot, Talbot, and Habijanac came to the Ranger Camp to explain the dynamics of the VO2 Expedition. Habijanac explained that he and his wife agreed to join VO2 without having previously met with Seedhouse and Nugent. Habijanac said he was concerned about the safety of the team. Methot and Talbot thought they should abandon the climb.

Habijanac said the group had taken a short mountaineering course, and he became concerned during the course when Nugent and Seedhouse displayed very little knowledge in mountaineering skills. The Ranger Patrol's collective opinion was that they demonstrated poor expedition behavior and mountaineering skills to climb Denali safely.

On May 14, Moore met with Seedhouse and explained that the VO2 Expedition should abort their climb because of safety concerns. Seedhouse was upset. He said the climb was sponsored by Simon Fraser University and the money given to him would have to be paid back.

On May 15, the entire VO2 team abandoned their climb. They were assisted by the GT Expedition to Basecamp.

FALL ON SNOW, FATIGUE, INADEQUATE EQUIPMENT
Alaska, Mount McKinley, West Buttress

On May 16 at 1840, Christoph Haider (24) fell from below Denali Pass while descending the West Buttress route. Ranger Kevin Moore and others witnessed the fall and responded to the scene where they assessed and stabilized Haider. Moore and Volunteer Ranger Jay Patterson determined he had suffered head injuries including a possible broken nose as well as a possible femur fracture. Haider was alert and able to move his toes; it was unclear if he had lost consciousness during the fall. Haider and Moore were short-hauled via the Lama helicopter from 17,000 feet to the 7,200 foot base camp where Haider was loaded into the Lama and evacuated to Talkeetna. A Lifeguard helicopter then took Haider to Providence Hospital in Anchorage, where his condition was given as stable. He had suffered a broken nose and lacerations to the head and face. His leg injury was diagnosed as an open knee joint, an injury caused by Haider's crampon, and a fractured ankle.

Analysis

This incident has many of the components of a classic Mount McKinley accident. Haider was descending after a long and tiring summit day. In addition, he was unroped and using only his ski poles instead of an ice ax. The terrain he fell on is considerably steeper and more exposed than he had just traveled on above Denali Pass. Numerous accidents have occurred on this traverse and despite having specifically warned this expedition about the hazards associated with, it they are yet another group to underestimate the danger this area presents.

FALL INTO CREVASSE
Alaska, Mount McKinley, Northwest Fork, Kahiltna Glacier

On May 13, The Velvet Underground Expedition, Courtland Shafer (33) and Glenn and Morrison (40) began their climb of Denali's West Rib. On May 24, Shafer and Morrison were camped at 11,000 feet near the base of the route. Shafer and Morrison had decided to abandon their climb and return to Basecamp. They left their camp at 1300, and descended towards the upper icefall of the Northeast Fork. There were two feet of new snow, and they followed a faint trail that sloped down hill about 15 degrees.

Shafer and Morrison were aware of the crevasse danger and were traveling with the rope tight between them. Shafer was leading and probing with ski poles (baskets on), as they crossed the glacier west to east. Shafer was tied directly into a waist harness and carried some coils of rope, and a 65-pound pack.

Shafer fell through a bridge and down into the crevasse. Shafer struck the wall of the crevasse three times before coming to rest 20 feet deep. Morrison who was ready for something to happen tried to arrest the fall by assuming a face down position. Shafer's weight pulled Morrison down, approximately 15 feet towards the crevasse opening. Morrison was able to set an anchor, but was unable to establish communication with Shafer. Shafer attached his pack to the rope with an ascender and waited about 10 minutes before ascending the rope towards the surface. Morrison assisted by dropping a loop of rope to Shafer, and rigging a "C" pulley system.

Shafer was injured by striking the wall of the crevasse, and sustained a contused elbow, cracked ribs, and a torn rotator cuff. Shafer climbed out and onto the surface, where both men tried to pull the pack up and over the lip of the crevasse. The pack was attached to the rope by only one of it's loops and it blew apart just as they were about to land it. The pack fell back down into the crevasse. The pack contained the tent, radio and Shafer's personal gear.

The crevasse extrication took an hour and a half and left both men tired from the efforts. They did not attempt to retrieve the pack because of their physical condition. They spent the next 18 hours negotiating and judiciously probing their way through the upper icefall. They bivouacked at "Safe Camp" (9,500 feet) and on May 25, they hiked to 7,800 feet on the Kahiltna Glacier.

At 7,800 feet, they contacted a French/Belgian expedition who provided food, shelter, and a sleeping bag for them. A Park Service Ranger Patrol also contacted Shafer and Morrison at 7,800 feet and provided radio communication to Basecamp. They then hiked to Basecamp. Their air taxi provided them with a ride to Talkeetna, where Shafer was treated by a doctor.

Analysis
Shafer and Morrison performed a self-rescue and demonstrated self-sufficiency in the mountains. A few thoughts on what may have helped:
- Probe with the baskets off the ski poles, and use the poles as one long probe.
- Morrison could have set up a belay while Shafer probed ahead.
- When tying in, a chest harness should be included

SERAC FALL
Alaska, Mount Johnson, Ruth Gorge
On May 15, Seth Shaw (38) and Tim Wagner (34) checked into the Talkeetna Ranger Station and filled out a backcountry permit to climb Mount Johnson. They were flown into the Ruth Glacier, Denali National Park and Preserve by Talkeetna Air Taxi.

On May 16, Shaw and Wagner started their climb of Mount Johnson, climbing a ice gully located on the center of the buttress. They finished the climb on May 21 and returned to their base camp at the base of Mount Dickey. The weather remained inclement for the next six days, forcing them to remain in their tent.

On May 25 at 1930, Shaw and Wagner skied to the base of Mount Johnson and climbed to the base of a large serac icefall located on the east side of a couloir. The icefall had an ice-cave-type entrance at the bottom and with an over-hanging serac some 50 feet higher than the entrance.

At 2000, Wagner walked into the ice cave—about 20 feet wide and 50 feet long—and placed his ice picks into the wall. Shaw was outside the cave about 50 feet down slope from Wagner and had laid his tools down to use his camera. As Shaw was taking a picture, the serac above them came crashing down on top of them both, burying Shaw. Wagner was pinned down by an ice boulder and spent about 30 minutes digging out to free himself. Wagner shouted for Shaw and looked at the huge pile of ice boulders that were stacked up an estimated 20-30 feet on top of where he had last seen Shaw standing.

At 2030, after hastily searching for Shaw and aware that climbers were camped at the base of Mount Dickey, Wagner skied up the glacier to get help. He contacted Kelly Cordes, Scott Decapio, Jeff Hollenbaugh, and Bruce Miller. After talking with the climbers Wagner decided he should stay at their camp. Decapio skied to the mountain house attempting to radio out for help.

At 2330, Miller, Hollenbaugh, and Cordes skied seven miles down to the accident site to attempt to locate Shaw. They belayed each other to the debris site several times, but were unable to find anything but Shaw's two ice tools. They surmised that the wind blast from the ice falling onto the snow caused enough force to blow the ice tools down glacier. They found Shaw's skis that were marking the site and also a pack he had laid down-slope from where the debris pile was. They shouted numerous times calling Seth's name, but they never heard any responses.

At 0120, Miller, Hollenbaugh, and Cordes skied back to their campsite at the base of Mount Dickey. The trio later was able to radio to an air taxi and report the accident.

At 1110, a K2 Air Taxi reported the accident to the National Park Service at Talkeetna Ranger Station. Talkeetna Air Taxi was near the scene and landed at the base of Mount Dickey and picked up Wagner and flew him to Talkeetna, where he was treated for a leg fracture at the Talkeetna Sunshine Clinic. At 1302, the NPS Lama rescue helicopter flew to the accident site with NPS Mountaineering Rangers Roger Robinson & Scott Metcalfe aboard and Jim Hood as the pilot. At 1325, the Lama hovered over the accident site while the Rangers videoed the site and looked for any sign of life. It was determined that the accident site was and is too dangerous to ground search and that there was a zero chance of survival.

Analysis

This was an unfortunate accident that demonstrated the unforgiving nature of icefalls. The tragic incident also confirms again that even the most experienced climbers are vulnerable to accidents. Shaw worked as an avalanche forecaster, had years of climbing experience in Alaska, and was extremely knowledgeable regarding ice and snow. This accident site was and is an active zone of seracs constantly calving. There was new debris present when Shaw and Wagner arrived at the icefall. In fact, since the accident the site has had numerous collapses of ice burying the site deeper with debris piles.

It was Wagner's first trip to Alaska and he commented that he depended on Shaw for judgment calls regarding hazards on glaciers including crevasses and icefalls. It will never be known or understood why Shaw decided to go into this precarious area that was even too dangerous to conduct a ground search safely.

HAPE
Alaska, Mount McKinley, West Buttress
At 1000 on May 27, Richard Gustafson (34) and William Ross (45)—clients from two separate expeditions—were experiencing symptoms of High Altitude Pulmonary Edema (HAPE). Gustafson was with Alaska Denali Guiding and Ross was with American Alpine Institute. Evacuated by helicopter from the 17,200-foot high camp on Mount McKinley's West Buttress route, the National Park Service Lama helicopter transported Gustafson and Ross to the 7,200-foot Basecamp where they were assessed and transferred to an Air National Guard Pavehawk helicopter, which flew them to Alaska Regional Hospital in Anchorage.
Analysis
There is little doubt that Ross and Gustafson needed to descend. Given this, there is only a question of how best to accomplish the task. The National Park Service often must rely on information from rescuers on scene when making evacuation decisions. This is especially true where guides are concerned, since their experience and skills often mean they play an integral role in rescue operations. Given the extenuating circumstances of cold and the possibility of having to leave only one guide with the rest of their clients that confronted Bob Hornbein (head guide for ADG) and Michael Silitch (head guide for AAI), they made a reasonable decision when they requested a helicopter evacuation.

AMS, CLIMBING ALONE (PARTY SEPARATED), INEXPERIENCE
Alaska, Mount McKinley, West Buttress
The International Climbing Buddies Expedition, consisting of Ralph Nicholson, James Foutch and Brett Johnson (35), reached the 17,200-foot camp on May 27. On May 28, Nicholson and Foutch went to the summit. Johnson felt he needed another day of rest and decided to go the next day. On May 29 at 0600, Johnson departed for the summit alone. Nicholson and Foutch waited at the 17,200-foot camp until about 1930, and then descended to the 14,200-foot camp with the group's tent and stove.

At 2215, Nicholson and Foutch contacted Ranger Gordy Kito, stationed at the 14,200-foot camp. Nicholson and Foutch asked Kito to contact the 17,200-foot camp and ask if anyone had seen Johnson.

At 2220, Kito was contacted by Michael Maude of Team Rumpus, who reported that an Icelandic group had encountered a solo climber above Denali Pass who was disorientated and unsure of the descent. Maude stated that he also had encountered a solo climber above the Pass and was concerned about the individual's ability to descend safely from the Pass to 17,200 feet. Kito asked Maude to call back when he received more information regarding the individual, but believed that the climber was Johnson.

At 2245, two people were reported descending from Denali Pass. At 2300, Maude confirmed the second person was Johnson. At 2311, Kito was notified that Maude, Bill McCormick and John Race of Alpine Ascents International (AAI), and Steve Sivils would start up to assist.

At 2355, Maude witnessed the climber take a couple of short falls close to the bottom of the traverse near the rocks just as the team was approaching. At 0025, Kito was notified that Johnson had been "short-roped" back to the 17,200-foot camp. Dr. Gretchen Lenz of the Huskies-2 Expedition assessed Johnson, revealing slight ataxia due to exhaustion. He was treated with warm fluids and rest. He slept in a tent with another group that was camped at the 17,200-foot camp. On May 30 at 1250, Kito, Taysom, and Smith departed from the 14,200-foot camp to assist Johnson down from the point at which they came into contact with him. Johnson roped up with the Team Rumpus Expedition and descended the West Buttress to the base of Washburn's Thumb (16,800 feet), where he was met by Kito and Taysom, and short-roped down to the 14,200-foot camp.

On May 30 at 0930, Ranger Joe Reichert received a radio transmission from John Race at the 17,200-foot camp. Race stated that Sam Palsmeier (29) of the West Butt Bros. Expedition was suffering from AMS and possibly HAPE. Palsmeier had a pulse of 120, an oxygen saturation of 52 percent, was pale, and had audible rales.

At 1142 , Bill McCormick (AAI) and John Race (AAI) reported that Palsmeier was walking poorly. He was given 8 mg of Dexamethasone at that time. At 1150, Palsmeier (while on two liters-per-minute of oxygen) and his partner started down from the 17,200-foot camp with assistance from Race, McCormick, and Colby Jackson of the At a Medium Pace Expedition. Upon arrival at 16,200 feet, Taysom assessed Palsmeier and determined that he, along with his partner, were fit enough to descend the fixed ropes unattended. Kito's observations of Palsmeier just below 16,200 feet reconfirmed this assessment. Volunteer Kevin Smith, who was on the fixed lines at approximately 15,900 feet, decided to follow Palsmeier and his partner down the remainder of the fixed lines in the event that they needed any further assistance. Smith continued to 14,200 feet with the two climbers.

Analysis

Nicholson and Foutch had previously attempted the West Buttress in 1999 as clients and made it to 17,200 feet. The deterioration of the team may have stemmed from the fact that this group was made up of two distinct parties. Nicholson and Foutch had originally intended on climbing with a third member who canceled in April. Johnson was added around this time. Johnson had taken a mountaineering course in the spring, but had not been on McKinley. A party of three is definitely safer than a party of two when it comes to glacier travel. The addition of another member for the sake of increased numbers does not take into account the group dynamics and possible conflicts that might arise from a disparity in ability, goals, and commitment to the "team." In the past, climbing teams seemed to be organized from an association of friends or mutual acquaintances. With the introduction of the Internet and increased communication (e.g. chat rooms, e-mail, and other common interest web-sites) people are finding partners with the same goal, but without the knowledge of skills and personal interaction that comes with meeting people face to face and going climbing. A member of a team should have some sense of responsibility for the other member(s), otherwise the team members are little more than weight on the other end of the rope.

In the second incident, in sharp contrast to the first, Palsmeier and his partner quickly recognized that he was not acclimatizing. With the help of his partner and a few other climbers, Palsmeier was able to descend before his condition worsened. Early recognition and a quick descent is the best treatment for altitude-related illness.

RESPIRATORY DISTRESS
Alaska, Mount McKinley, West Buttress
On May 26, the Casade-Dacks Expedition of Ron Fridell (50), Sid Perkins, and Don Andrews (43) flew to the Kahiltna Glacier to begin their climb of the West Buttress of Mount McKinley. Over the next five days the group proceeded to the 11,000-foot camp. On June 1, the team made a carry to 13,500 feet, which is a popular strategy for the difficult move from 11,000 feet to 14,200 feet, and returned to the lower camp. On June 2, the group was climbing past Windy Corner en route to the 14,200-foot camp when Andrews began having trouble breathing. According to Fridell, Andrews slowed down noticeably, began resting more often and developed a productive cough. Andrews' respiratory distress became so alarming that the group stopped and Fridell continued to the 14,200-foot camp alone and without his pack in order to summon help. Fridell arrived at the NPS Ranger Camp at 2130 and reported the incident.

By 2154, Volunteer Rangers Denny Gignoux and Jay Mathers were on scene assessing Andrews and administering oxygen. With in five minutes Joe Conroy and Marty Kimble, Air National Guard Pararescuemen (PJ's), were also on scene working with Andrews, while Gignoux and Mathers prepared an anchor to begin lowering the patient for possible evacuation.

By 2215, the PJs had conferred with Dr. Peter Hackett about Andrews' condition and it was decided that he should be evacuated, so the helicopter was requested from Talkeetna. The decision was based on the patient's history of cauterized esophageal varacies that could rupture and cause serious internal bleeding if his respiratory distress continued or became more severe. Andrews was not responding as well as was expected to treatment with his personal inhaler and supplemental oxygen. He continued to be pale and cough up pink sputum.

At 2300, the NPS Lama rescue helicopter departed Talkeetna en route directly to Andrews. At this same time Chris Eng and Dan Howley (emergency hired climbers), departed camp with additional cylinders of oxygen. Upon their arrival at 2317, Eng and Howley replaced the existing oxygen and descended to 13,500 feet and prepared a landing zone for the helicopter. The Lama landed, the patient was put on board at 2339, and was on the ground at Basecamp at 2349.

Dr. Peter Hackett evaluated Andrews at Basecamp while waiting for the Air National Guard Pavehawk to arrive. At 0119 on June 3, Andrews was transported to Alaska Regional Hospital where he was seen and released.

PULMONARY EDEMA
Alaska, Mt. McKinley, West Buttress

While the incident with Andrews was unfolding at 13,500 feet, there was another incident developing at high camp—17,200 feet. The Black Ice Expedition, consisting of Sacha Friedlin (23) and Marie Cyr (24), were spending their third night at the 17,200-foot camp and Cyr had developed pulmonary edema. Ranger Gordy Kito was on scene at high camp with his Volunteer Patrol members Lance Taysom and Kevin Smith. Cyr's condition had deteriorated rapidly over the course of the evening. Taysom started her on oxygen and initially encouraged the team to rest. Because her condition was not improving, Kito conferred with the 14,200-foot camp and the Talkeetna Ranger Station. Since the weather was favorable and the Black Ice team was unable to have productive rest, it was decided that they should descend immediately. Departing 17,200 feet at 0223, Taysom and Smith accompanied Cyr and Friedlin to the 16,000-foot level, where they were met by Ranger Joe Reichert and Volunteer Jay Mathers and escorted down to the medical camp. While descending, Cyr remained on oxygen with a portable cylinder in her backpack. Cyr remained on oxygen and slept for the remainder of June 3 in the ranger medical tent. The oxygen and lower altitude aided Cyr's recovery. Her edema disappeared within two days. She remained at the 14,200-foot camp for over two more weeks before the team proceeded to ascend to Denali Pass and continue their traverse out to Wonder Lake.

(On a side note, Friedlin became only the third person to ever summit Mount McKinley, Mount Foraker and Mount Hunter all in the same season, and the first to do so after hiking in from Petersville.)

Analysis

It could be said that Andrews used poor judgment in making the decision to return to high altitude with his medical condition. Other than that, his team used sound strategy during their ascent and Andrews' evacuation was based on an emergency condition that was not being reduced on the mountain.

The second incident was not related to poor judgment. Cyr only moved to high camp after normal acclimatization at the 14,200-foot level. Her pulmonary edema developed quickly, as happens on occasion to people at high altitude. To their credit, they descended under their own power with minimal assistance with their gear from NPS Rangers.

FALLING ICE
Alaska, Mount McKinley, Mount Johnson

At 1500 on June 8, Jeff Benowitz (30) and partner Chris Turiano (29) started climbing a new route on the East Buttress of Mt. Johnson. Turiano was leading approximately 100 feet up the route when falling ice struck his belayer,

Benowitz, giving him moderate injuries. Turiano did not cause the ice to fall. Benowitz lowered Turiano to the ground and they both skied back to their basecamp. Turiano provided basic first aid to Benowitz and stomped a "HELP" message into the snow.

At 1700, an air taxi flight spotted the "HELP" message and informed the Talkeetna Ranger Station. At 1733, Talkeetna Air Taxi pilot Paul Roderick reported that he had landed at the site, described the climbers' conditions, and said he would be transporting Benowitz back to Talkeetna. Turiano stayed on the Ruth Glacier. Roderick and Benowitz arrived in Talkeetna at 1910. Park personnel Dave Kreutzer took Benowitz to the Sunshine Clinic, where he received eight stitches to his forehead. He also had sustained minor bruising to his left shoulder.

HAPE
Alaska, Mount McKinley, West Buttress
Charles Grey (40) of the Unfinished Business Expedition (party of 2), reported symptoms of HAPE to the 14,200-foot Ranger Camp on Mount McKinley at midnight on June 9. Grey was ataxic with an oxygen saturation of 61 percent. He was placed on oxygen and improved enough to descend with assistance at 1300. Grey descended on oxygen, reaching the 11,000-foot camp at 1700 with the help of Park Service Volunteers Denny Gignoux and Jay Mathers. After several days of rest at the 11,000-foot camp, Grey was able to ascend and continue his climb without incident.

Analysis
Grey had ascended to 19,000 feet on a previous climb of Denali without any altitude problems. On this particular climb he ascended to the 14,000-foot level in five days, which is generally the minimum recommended. Considering his previous ascent this climb should have gone without incident. This scenario goes to show that anyone can get HAPE and with an early diagnosis and rapid descent, it might be possible to reascend and continue the climb.

ILLNESS—ABDOMINAL PAIN, MISCOMMUNICATION—FAILURE TO DISCLOSE MEDICAL CONDITION
Alaska, Mount McKinley, West Buttress
On June 9 at the 16,700-foot level of the West Buttress of Mt. McKinley, Lai Yuk Man (38) collapsed from abdominal distress and was unable to move due to severe pain. The Park Service coordinated a team to lower Man down to the 14,200-foot camp where he arrived at 0730. Dr. Peter Hackett, Dr. Donner and Nurse Practitioner George Rodway immediately examined Man. Upon examination, Man was no longer experiencing pain in his abdomen. Man was administered intravenous fluids and oxygen for the next 24 hours and released on June 11. In further analysis of patient history, Man disclosed that he had experienced similar pain twice a year for the past six years and indicated the medical profession did not know the cause. None of his party indicated they knew he suffered this medical condition. Man's condition stabilized and he flew out without assistance on June 13.

Analysis

This type of medical emergency, involving an expedition member who does not disclose previous medical conditions to other expedition members, has become more common in recent years on Denali. This places all involved personnel in harm's way. This issue raises a series of ethical questions: Should such an individual be allowed to climb in the first place? Should someone like this—who jeopardizes so many people—be fined and escorted off the mountain? Or, should the NPS allow the situation to remain status quo? What most bothered the author of this report is that this Hong Kong climber wanted to go back up after a few days of rest at 14,200 feet. He was told he could not, under the authority that he would be "Creating a Hazardous Condition" (36 CFR 2.34[4]). It seems unfortunate but likely that Mr. Man would rather have died than come back without tagging the summit.

FALL ON SNOW
Alaska, Mount McKinley, Denali Pass

On June 10 at 1945, Lev Sarkisov (61) of the Denali–2000 Khalatian Expedition (D2K) was descending unroped from Denali Pass on Mt. McKinley when he stumbled at the 17,400-foot level and fell 400 feet. Sarkisov sustained numerous broken ribs and was stabilized at the 17,200-foot high camp. On May 12, a large rescue team lowered him to the 14,200-foot camp where he was evacuated by military Chinook helicopter to Talkeetna. From Talkeetna he was flown to the Alaska Regional Hospital in Anchorage where he was diagnosed with eight fractures on six ribs.

Analysis

This was the second rescue this season where a European climber fell descending the Denali Pass traverse unroped, using only ski poles. Both men were fortunate that they were not killed, though both required extensive rescue operations. The D2K party was adamant that Lev Sarkisov be flown off from the 17,200-foot high camp without delay, regardless of the weather conditions. They learned very quickly that the Park Service does not provide a European-style helicopter rescue service and that Denali's weather dictates everything. For the past 20 years the Park Service has tried to educate climbers with reference to the exposure of the Denali Pass traverse and our inability to provide instant rescues. There has been some headway made regarding Europeans who frequently acknowledge Park Service concerns, and many more are now descending with an ice ax, as witnessed by this author. Those who refuse to listen and end up being rescued create hazardous conditions for all rescuers involved. The Park Service and many volunteer rescuers are frustrated with this attitude.

AMS—ASCENDING TOO FAST, CLIMBING "ALONE"—BUT DEPENDING UPON OTHERS
Alaska, Mount McKinley, Denali Pass

On June 25 at 1940, Ranger Meg Perdue received a radio call from Volunteer Ranger Karen Hilton at the 17,200-foot high camp regarding a solo climber who was non-ambulatory on the traverse from Denali Pass. A guide there relayed to Hilton that he had been contacted via CB radio by a private expedition, Spirit of El Rancho, who were very concerned about this climber, Russell Worthington (29). He had been traveling with them to the summit and had vomited on the summit ridge several times and appeared ataxic. Now, upon their descent, they relayed he was unable to walk and was again vomiting. Worthington's position was reported to be halfway between Denali Pass and the rock band that initiates the traverse above the 17,200-foot camp.

At 1947, the Spirit of El Rancho Expedition was recontacted directly by Hilton, and confirmed that Worthington was exhausted and unable to walk, but that he was alert and oriented. They were instructed to give him fluids and await further assistance. At 1951, Hilton was able to contact two other Volunteer Rangers, Josie Garton and Dave Shuman, who were descending from the summit and were currently at Denali Pass. At 2000, Hilton had secured the assistance of three guides, Bob Hornbein, Scott Raynor and Kirby Spangler, and was preparing to ascend with oxygen to meet them. At this time, Ranger Perdue also contacted Talkeetna and relayed the situation, gave current weather observations, and requested the helicopter be put on stand-by.

At 2022, Garton and Shuman reached Worthington's location and assessed his condition. Worthington's condition had already improved somewhat with fluids and food, and though he showed signs of Acute Mountain Sickness, he was not ataxic. They determined that he could be safely short-roped down to camp.

At 2204, they arrived at the 17,200-foot camp, Worthington's condition was reassessed and he was found to be doing well. He rested at camp that night, was checked again in the morning, and descended to the 14,200-foot camp on his own.

Analysis

Two important and intractable issues present themselves in this case. One is the relative rapidity of Worthington's ascent and the second is the problem of "solo" climbers asking to rope up with other expeditions on the mountain. Worthington had been on Mt. McKinley only 10 days by the date of his summit bid. He had actually ascended to 17,200 feet on day nine, but returned to 14,200 feet when he developed a severe headache. There is always a question in cases such as this if a slower ascent rate might have resulted in the whole situation being avoided. In interviews with members of the Spirit of El Rancho Expedition and Worthington, it came to light that Worthington had asked if he could rope up with them on summit day to which they agreed. They had become very concerned about Worthington near the summit and wanted to turn him around, but did not feel comfortable telling him that since he was not part of their expedition. They also felt a certain responsibility for him since they had agreed to rope up with him and, thus, did not want to leave him on his own. For Worthington's part, in interviewing him, he admitted that he did not believe he was properly acclimatized and stated, "I knew I would get sick."

When queried as to why he would put another expedition in the position of dealing with this, he said, "I didn't think it would be a problem." Since he had done things like this before (rapid ascents where he felt ill), he thought he could handle it and did not expect the group to react the way they did. Worthington maintained throughout that he did not need the assistance and never would have called for it.

The problem still remains that one individual's difficulties invariably become the concerns of others in an environment such as Mount McKinley. It is only when everyone takes very seriously the need for self-sufficiency that the risks can be minimized for all concerned.

(Editor's Note: All the reports from Denali National Park were edited by Daryl Miller, South District Chief Ranger in Denali National Park. The reports he worked from were written by Rangers Roger Robinson, Kevin Moore, and others.)

AVALANCHE—UNSAFE CONDITIONS, WEATHER, POOR POSITION, INADEQUATE EQUIPMENT—NO ICE AX
Alaska, Chugach State Park, Flat Top Mountain

On Saturday November 11, Nick Coltman (36) and his dog Boozer decided to get some exercise and do a fast hike up Flat Top Mountain via the back side— not a standard route, but one Coltman had traveled many times before. Walking was easy because the snow was less than ankle deep most of the way and the tundra was blown bare in many places. The crux of the route is the last 100 meters to the ridge where the gully narrows and steepens through an S-shaped curve. The snow conditions as Coltman entered this segment around noon were different (i.e., more unstable) than any of the previous route. Within a few steps, the snow broke beneath him and sent him falling out of control down the gully. Scrape marks from his finger tips were found in the old bed surface where he had attempted to arrest his fall (he carried no ice ax). Coltman slid an estimated 60 meters down the gully at high speed (estimated at 35-45 mph). As the avalanche gained momentum and distance, it entrained additional unstable snow on the surface. Where the gully opened onto a 35-degree scree slope, he was carried in soft slab debris another 120 meters. In the process he was banged against many boulders lodged in the frozen scree and his dog was scraped and bruised. Debris in the runout zone was less than 30 centimeters deep by 50 meters wide by 200 meters long. The debris extended about 60 meters beyond Coltman in a shallow arc.

Coltman was found in a vertical alignment lying on his back, arms out, legs twisted with his feet up-slope and head down-slope. His hands and head were bare. All 10 fingers were white with frostbite, his head covered with blood. In his right hand, he held a cell phone. He was conscious of his situation, mildly hypothermic, complained of difficulty breathing, and had no feeling in the lower portion of his body. He said later that he knew he would die if he could not reach his cell phone in the bottom of his pack. Somehow, with one lung collapsed and the other partially collapsed, a broken back and paralyzed legs, and frozen fingers, he managed to remove his backpack, retrieve his cell phone, dial 911, and describe his location and predicament.

Rescuers from multiple agencies and groups responded immediately to the Glen Alps parking lot in Chugach State Park. Within minutes, a Life Flight helicopter lifted two paramedics and an avalanche/mountain rescue specialist to the top of Flat Top Mountain, the nearest landing zone. They down-climbed to the site. When the first rescuer arrived approximately 45 minutes after the 911 call, Coltman was lucid, uncomfortable, resolved to stay alive, and worried about his fingers. He said he was sure his back was broken. A primary and secondary survey was performed, heat packs and clothing added, and a snow platform constructed horizontal to the slope. Coltman was carefully moved onto the platform and stabilized with whatever gear was available.

It was clear from the beginning that the most expeditious means of evacuating Coltman would be by using a helicopter sling-hoist. Unfortunately, the Life Flight helicopter was not sling-hoist equipped. In anticipation of this, a Pavehawk helicopter was requested from the 210th Air National Guard. The request was approved, but they would not be able to launch for an hour at the earliest. Preparations were made for a ground evacuation which would require belaying the litter from equalizing anchor systems using rescuers as anchor points (no solid natural anchors existed). This was not the preferred option because of the additional time and exposure demanded of the gravely injured patient. Meanwhile, Coltman was becoming increasingly hypothermic and having difficulty breathing.

Eventually, the Pavehawk arrived on site and, as the two PJ's were lowered with a litter on the winch cable, they started to spin. As the length of the cable increased, the rate of the spin increased. By the time they were nearing the ground, they were spinning out-of-control directly over the heads of the ground team, who were hunkered down in the 75-90 mph winds (from the helicopter rotor wash) trying to keep the patient from blowing away. Two ground team members were hit by the spinning legs and litter, and one was knocked a short distance down-slope. This was a near-miss accident that could have resulted in several injuries to rescuers and/or death to the patient. Placement of personnel using a sling hoist in the mountain environment is difficult at best, especially with blowing snow and no radio communication between air and ground teams.

Within 10 minutes the patient was secured in the litter and hoisted out with one PJ. Then the second PJ was lifted out and the patient transported to Providence Hospital. Ground teams cleaned up the area and headed back to the staging area. When Coltman arrived at Providence Hospital, he reportedly had a core temperature of 85 degrees F.

Analysis

Terrain, weather, snow stability, and human factors conspired to cause this accident. The terrain was steep and exposed. It afforded poor anchoring for the thin, unstable slab created during the preceding night's snowfall and wind. What would be considered a minor instability of little consequence on a less exposed slope became critically important in the more exposed gully. When a small slab dish-plated out from underneath the climber, it sent him tumbling over rough terrain and, without an ice ax, he was unable to arrest the fall. Overconfidence, based upon experience on the same route under different conditions, may also have played a part. In summary, this was a minor slab release in a high-consequence terrain. Luck, the cell phone, the helicopters, the rescuers, and Coltman's will power and toughness all contributed to his survival.

(Source: Doug Fesler and Jill Fredston, Alaska Mountain Safety Center, Inc.)
(Editor's Note: This hiking incident fell into the climbing/mountaineering category once Coltman entered the gully containing unstable snow conditions. It should be noted that Boozer was only slightly injured.)

STRANDED—RAPPEL ROPE TOO SHORT
Arizona, Camelback Mountain
On March 15, a person who wishes to remain anonymous was attempting to rappel from a rock face that is 400 feet high. He started rappelling, and when he got close to the end of his rope, he realized he was still 150 feet from the ground. His partner realized he was in trouble and called 911. The Fire Department came to his rescue. He was not injured—except for his ego—as the rescue was video-taped and shown on three major television stations. (Source: Kathy Reichert, Park Manager, City of Phoenix)
(Editor's Note: This is by far the largest error in estimating the length of rope needed for a rappel. Enough said.)

RAPPEL ERROR—FALL ON ROCK
Arizona, Tucson, Papago Buttes
On August 10 at 7:00 pm, Kyle Brown (22) plunged 50 feet off a cliff at Papago Buttes while teaching kids from his church how to rappel.

It took rescue crews about an hour to reach Brown. Fire officials said that Brown's head injuries suppressed his breathing, and by the time firefighters reached him, he did not have a pulse. He was admitted to Scottsdale Healthcare Osborn Hospital, where he was later pronounced dead.

Analysis
Police and fire officials said they were not sure what caused Kyle Brown to fall that night, but they think that Brown was anchored and starting his descent when the accident occurred. Bob Khan, a deputy chief with the Phoenix Fire Department, said they were not sure whether a knot used to support Brown failed or whether he lost his footing.

Rescue crews frequently respond to calls involving the park for stuck or injured rappellers, but this is the first fatal accident there in years. The majority of calls are to Camelback and Squaw Peak, with the rest divided among North Mountain, South Mountain and Papago Buttes. According to Khan, the problem with Papago is that the rock there is not like Squaw Peak or Camelback. It is clay-like, and it is inviting because the rocks are rounded. They are deceivingly high and pretty easy to climb. (Source: From a report in *The Arizona Republic* by Christina Leonard.)

FALL ON SNOW, INADEQUATE EQUIPMENT, PLACED NO PROTECTION, NO HARD HAT, EXCEEDING ABILITIES
California, Castle Crags Wilderness
On March 23, John Stafford (17), who had some training and experience in rock climbing, made climbing the focus of his senior project. Ian Smith (18), who had no climbing experience, came to take photos of John. After taking the

trail to the top of Castle Dome, they descended a snow couloir, attached to each other by webbing tied to their belts. (They wore no harnesses and had no ice axes.) One fell, bringing down the other.

During the fall, Ian's belt released and he continued to tumble 300 feet to the creek drainage. He suffered a fracture to the lumbar vertebrae and a punctured lung. He spent the night out and was then rescued by the Highway Patrol helicopter and flown to Mercy Mt. Shasta. John Stafford stopped in a moat 80 feet below the fall and died of head and spinal injuries. His body was recovered by Climbing Rangers and a helicopter.

Analysis
Although the couloir itself is not technically difficult, the lack of appropriate climbing equipment, as well as the vertical exposure, added to the danger.

It should be noted that the helicopter rescue and the recovery were very dangerous. (Source: Eric White and Matt Hill, USFS Climbing Rangers)

WEATHER, EXPOSURE, FAILURE TO TURN BACK
California, Mount Shasta
Early Monday morning April 10, Craig Hiemstra (38) and John "Zippo" Miksits (45), both experienced climbers, set out from the Bunny Flat Trailhead in beautiful weather to climb Mt. Shasta via Cascade Gulch. John and Craig had never climbed together before. They had made acquaintance at the trailhead with two other climbers, who then went with them. Their first camp was in Hidden Valley.

April 11 brought more beautiful weather, with a slight increase in winds, and both groups made their next camp at Lake Sisson, in a sheltered depression at the Shasta/Shastina saddle about 11,500 feet. That afternoon the winds increased, but nobody was alarmed. John mentioned the high, thin clouds he had been noticing, and Craig responded that the barometric pressure had remained constant and stable for the past four hours. Agreeing that there was no need to worry, the pair made plans for a 1:00 a.m. departure for the summit. The other two climbers decided that a summit attempt was out, due to their limited technical expertise, and that a ski descent from the saddle would be their plan for morning.

When they went to sleep, the temperature was around 25 degrees F, winds were around 35 mph, and the moon was visible through a thin layer of clouds. The winds continued throughout the night and the moon soon became disguised. Dawn brought whiteout conditions and winds up to 65 mph through the saddle.

On 12 April at 8:00 a.m., the two climbers who remained at the saddle received a radio call from John: "We are descending from summit, are at 11,900 feet, but can't find camp. Can you call the weather service and see if this is going to stick around."

The two at the saddle agreed and scheduled to make radio contact again in 20 minutes. Upon attempting to reach John and Craig after that interval, they received no response, nor did they ever again establish contact, despite repeated attempts. The pair remained at the saddle as long as they could, then descended because the high winds were starting to rip apart their two-season tent, while continuing attempts to contact by radio.

John and Craig were reported missing on April 13 when a check of the Bunny Flat Trailhead revealed that John's vehicle was still in the parking lot. A major search operation ensued, involving two California Guard Blackhawks, US Air Force Pavehawk, USFS CWN Bell Jet Ranger, and CHP A-Star. Over-the-snow vehicles and skiers were used on the days when weather conditions made flying impossible. On April 15, Craig's body was discovered without gloves or ice ax at an elevation of approximately 10,300 feet in Cascade Gulch. Injuries were consistent with a headfirst fall in soft snow (fractured cervical vertebra), and death had been instantaneous.

On April 19, during the search for John, a California Guard UH-60 Blackhawk crashed at 11,600 feet near Cascade Gulch, just below the Shasta/Shastina saddle. The helicopter rolled at least once and came to rest on its side, yet those on board—four Guardsmen, a reporter, and two Climbing Rangers—sustained only minor injuries. The party descended together through clouds to a helispot. The Guard crew and reporter were evacuated later that day by another Guard Blackhawk. The Climbing Rangers skied out to Bunny Flat through hazardous avalanche conditions, continuing to search.

John's body remained buried by snow and undiscovered until the Memorial Day weekend, when we found his remains at approximately 11,500 feet on the north side of the saddle. Subsequent autopsy revealed a dislocated wrist, pulmonary edema (associated with either the altitude or the terminal stages of hypothermia), a heart condition, and the probable cause of death was listed as hypothermia. Seventy-five feet above John's body, a meager bivouac site was found. Buried by almost two feet of snow, and almost directly beneath John's body was most of their gear, including water and food, packs, wands, and Craig's gloves and ax, laid out in an organized fashion. The sleeping bags and cooking gear were gone, however.

Analysis

Although there has been much speculation, we will never know for certain exactly what happened up there after the last radio contact. We do know that John and Craig were hit by an extremely violent and prolonged winter storm with winds in excess of 60 mph, which dropped two feet of snow in 24 hours, and which, by the end of the search, had deposited over six feet of new snow on the mountain. The presence of Craig's body in Cascade Gulch suggests that he may have been on his way to get help for John, and suffered a fatal fall.

The fact that John and Craig had never climbed together previously should also be noted. While we will never know if this was a contributing factor in this accident, knowledge of your partner, and of yourself, in critical situations, can sometimes make a difference in the outcome.

The bottom line is this: In the high mountains, even ones we are familiar with, there is but one season: Winter. When a big storm moves in, circumstances can rapidly compound into a potentially fatal situation. High winds, zero visibility, and heavy snowfall all can combine to disorient and incapacitate the most able climber. Add a physical problem like an injury sustained in a fall or AMS, HAPE or HACE, and the odds rapidly mount against us. Preparation and awareness are our closest allies against those odds. I miss my friend. Be careful out there! (Source: Bruce Binder, friend of victim and searcher. Report reviewed by other search volunteers: E. Holland, M. Golay, J. Burns, J. Huber, J. Keeney, and Dave Nicholson, Incident Commander)

FALLING ROCK
California, Yosemite Valley, El Capitan

On April 24, Cam Lawson (30) was leading the 6th pitch of Iron Hawk, a Grade VI route on El Capitan. This pitch starts on the big ledge from which the El Cap Tree grows. Jason Kraus (29) was belaying from the ledge, using a GriGri clipped to his harness. He was clipped directly to the bolted anchor with his daisy chains.

After scrambling up a 4th class section, Cam made several hook moves on loose rock, then he placed some pieces to reach a crack system below a 15-foot roof. He placed a cam behind a big expanding flake, and when the piece shifted under his weight, he yelled to Jason to be "heads up" because of the unstable rock. A minute before, Jason had removed his helmet to adjust his headband and wipe the sweat from his forehead. When Cam yelled, Jason reached for the helmet but fumbled it, and it fell onto the ledge, out of reach.

Cam placed another piece behind the same flake; when he weighted it, a slab about 1x6x13 feet broke away from the flake, releasing Cam and his uppermost pieces. The falling slab hit a small ledge 20 feet above Jason and burst into fragments.

Jason saw everything coming his way and reached for the brake-end of the rope, but he only had time to hunker down close to the anchor and cover his head with his free arm. He remembers being hit by at least three pieces, roughly the size of softballs, before he was knocked unconscious. When he awoke a moment later, he was hanging from his daisy chains, unable to move his arms or legs, but he recovered in less than 30 seconds.

One of their ropes was shredded by the rocks, another was cut in a few places, but the third was unscathed. The lead rope was severed five to ten feet behind the GriGri, but the device had done its job, engaging the rope automatically and stopping Cam after he had fallen 20-25 feet. He had only minor scrapes and contusions on his lower right leg where the loose flake had hit him while he and the flake were falling together.

Jason tied the good rope onto what was left of the belay rope and lowered Cam to the belay ledge using a Munter Hitch. By rappelling on single lines and passing knots, they were able to get themselves and their gear to the ground.

The rocks had missed Jason's head, but not his neck. X-rays at the Yosemite clinic and later at home showed that he had suffered a chipped spinous process on a cervical vertebra and a compression fracture of the T-7 vertebra. Nevertheless, he was back climbing within a couple of months.

Analysis

Thin exfoliation slabs are characteristic of granite. You can see the scars of similar rockfalls all around the Valley, and it is pretty difficult to climb walls without exposing yourself to this risk.

Jason: "The quality of granite in the vicinity of the NA Wall is relatively poor for El Cap. It's no wonder the wall overhangs there more than anywhere else, and no wonder the roof above us was so big. I've heard stories of border-line epics on routes like the NA Wall, because even though the climbing is relatively straight forward, the darker dioritic rock is so loose in places that typically solid piton placements become suspect. You often have no way to judge how solid an expanding flake is. In fact, Dale Bard told me that when he did the first ascent of Iron Hawk 20 years ago, he thought Cam's flake would fall off then. But, if you back off every time a piece shifts, you'll never get up a wall and should probably choose a different hobby.

"A helmet definitely would have protected my head if I'd been hit there. I'm pretty damn lucky that the rocks missed my head and that they didn't do more damage to my neck. Cam and I still ruminate over how lucky we both were... that the lead rope wasn't cut above the GriGri, that the GriGri held, that neither of us was crushed by the rock, that we were able to get ourselves down. What a silly sport." (Source: John Dill, NPS Ranger, Yosemite National Park)

FALL ON ROCK– INADEQUATE HAULING SYSTEM
California, Yosemite Valley, El Capitan

On May 2, Jeff (40) and Don (20) climbed the first two pitches of Zenyatta Mondatta (VI 5.7 A5) on El Capitan. They hauled most of their gear and returned to the Valley for the night, leaving their ropes fixed in place. The 60-meter lead rope, anchored at the top of pitch two, was 30 feet short of the ground, so they tied on the haul line to get the rest of the way down; the rest of the haul line lay piled on the ground. Since both pitches overhang, the lines hung free all the way from the anchor.

The next morning Jeff climbed the fixed ropes, intent on hauling the last load of gear. When he reached the anchor, he clipped his two daisy chains to the bolts and got off the rope, standing on footholds.

He set up a basic hauling system: He rigged the fixed lead rope through a pulley and pulled all the slack rope up from the ground, through the pulley, until he felt the weight of the haul bag. He held the rope from the haul bag in place with an upside down ascender on the haul bag side of the pulley; as the load came up, the ascender would capture its progress. Now all the slack in the system, about 160 feet of lead rope, hung in an 80-foot long loop between the pulley and where the lead rope was tied to the anchor.

Jeff attached his other ascender to the rope on the loop side of the pulley, clipped the ascender to his harness, and got to work, hauling in short segments by pushing out from the wall. He also disconnected his daisy chains to give himself more range. Now he was supported by his feet on the holds and the resistance of the haul bag. After getting the bag up 40-50 feet and passing the knot through the pulley, he got tired of the repetition and decided to counterbalance haul (i.e., he would ride the rope down on his side of the pulley while the bag came up on the other side), as he had often done with heavy loads in the past.

With his single hauling ascender clipped on the line (he was not even tied in short), he stepped off. But he had overlooked two facts: He weighed 170 pounds, while the bag—just portaledges and clothing—weighed no more than 50 pounds. Don, standing on the ground, heard a "ziiiiiip!" and lookezd up to see Jeff rocketing down the wall, passing the haul bag like two cars in a game of chicken. Jeff said later that the weight discrepancy never struck him as significant.

If nothing had intervened, Jeff would have fallen until the haul bag slammed into the pulley or he reached the bottom of the loop (which lengthened as he fell). Either case would have sent him about 200 feet (plus stretch), possibly striking the ground or loading his ascender to the breaking point. But the loop had twisted below him, and it entangled him as he fell. He stopped, held in place by a huge wad of rope cinched tightly around his lower legs, hanging upside down 120 feet in the air and 15 feet from the wall. The bag hung 30-40 feet below the pulley, but both sides of the loop were partially supporting him.

Jeff struggled to get himself upright and get the tension off his legs by tying prusiks on the rope with shoe laces and webbing, but they kept slipping. The ropes soon cut off the circulation in one leg. He developed a headache and felt like he was blacking out. After an hour of thrashing around, he asked Don to get help from the Park Service.

Leading two A4 pitches to reach him would have taken the SAR team more time than Jeff could spare, so they used a line gun to shoot a cord up through the loop, where Jeff could grab it. He pulled up a rope and a pair of ascenders; he anchored that rope to his own by attaching the ascenders to one side of the loop supporting him. Team member Scott Burk started up the line, but the haul bag went up and Scott went down. Jeff had clipped the ascenders to the pulley side of the loop! He switched them to the anchored side and Scott climbed up to him quickly.

Scott anchored himself on the lead rope just above Jeff and tied him off. After a few minutes he managed to raise Jeff enough to get him untangled, then he lowered him to the ground with the NPS rope through a descender. At one point Scott noticed an ascender hanging free from Jeff's harness. Jeff had apparently removed it from the line during his struggles, leaving him completely dependent on the snarl around his legs.

Jeff had been dangling there for three hours or more. When he got down, the muscles in one foot were paralyzed because of nerve damage. After being examined at El Cap Meadow by the ambulance crew and the park physician, he refused further treatment, even though he could barely walk. He eventually recovered the use of his foot.

Analysis

On the one hand, this incident should need no analysis. Jeff had climbed over 60 walls in his career. He knew the importance of a secure tie-in, and he should have known the weight of the haul bag. He was used to hauling heavy loads this way and the consequences this time simply did not occur to him. (There are safe ways to haul light loads, using yourself as a counterbalance.) He also did not have a chest harness, prusik slings, or other gear that would have made a self-rescue easier, and he did not think to tie three-wrap prusiks or other ascender hitches, when his two-wrap prusiks slipped.

There is another factor, however. Everyone at the scene said Jeff reeked of alcohol—Scott smelled it from at least 10 feet away as he climbed the rope. Jeff was belligerent with rescuers and medics. He claimed that he had had only one drink—vodka—that morning, and insisted that he was dead sober on the wall. No legal action was taken against him.

Regardless of his state of sobriety, Jeff came close to dying in several ways, and getting him to safety put Scott at more than normal risk when he relied on Jeff's rigging. (Source: John Dill, NPS Ranger, Yosemite National Park)
(Editor's Note: We are reminded of the famous Buster Keaton comedy routine involving a pulley, rope, and wooden bucket of bricks...)

FALL ON ROCK, PLACED INADEQUATE PROTECTION
California, Mount Whitney
On May 15, Graeme Taylor (39) and Keith Reid (37), both experienced climbers, were in the Giant Staircase of the East Face route on Mt. Whitney. Graeme was about 40 feet out on lead when a snow mushroom he was standing on collapsed. Graeme fell 40 feet to one of the stairs. He briefly lost consciousness and suffered injuries so that he was unable to climb further. Keith placed him in a bivy sack, tied him in, and solo climbed to the top. He descended via the trail and notified the Kern County Sheriff.

Analysis
Place pro even when your skill level might not require it, especially in questionable terrain. Err on the side of caution when on mixed terrain. Both climbers were wearing helmets. Graeme's helmet was severely damaged in the fall, but it probably saved his life. (Source: Werner Hueber, China Lake Mountain Rescue Group)
(Editor's Note: There was one other incident reported from Mount Whitney. A 64-year-old man lost control when glissading, resulting in a fractured fibula. Though he had 48 years of experience, he still chose to wear crampons, and when he hit a hard patch of snow, his right crampon caught.)

FALL ON ROCK, INADEQUATE BELAY, POOR COMMUNICATION
California, Yosemite Valley, Lower Yosemite Falls
On June 24, Raj Dhingra (39), my brother Hugh (34), and I—Dan Sakols (37)—decided to tackle Commitment (three pitches, 5.9), one of the "Five Open Books" west of Lower Yosemite Falls. We got an early start to avoid the crowd and finished the first two pitches, both 5.8, with no complications.

Hugh led the third pitch, which starts with 5.9 moves around the right side of a big roof, then finishes up a right-facing 5.8 corner. After Hugh climbed out of sight at the top it was impossible to communicate, even by shouting.

There were light tugs on the rope, but we had not prearranged a signal, so I was not sure if he was still setting up the anchor or wanted me to climb. Raj and I waited for 10 minutes as another party came up behind us, then I got some solid tugs in response to mine, and I was comfortable starting up.

It was nearly midday now and the sun was hot. My pack—with water and descent shoes—was heavy, and the roof moves were hard, so I was tired by the time I finished the pitch. When I got to the top and it was my turn to belay, I looked for a way to make communications a little easier for Raj.

Hugh had anchored to the nearest live oak, about 20 feet up and left of the top of the corner, and had sat next to it to belay me. Being so far back from the edge of the cliff had caused the communication problem, so I decided to stand near the edge, on a slab just right of the corner, where I could see down the pitch and talk to Raj.

I was perhaps five feet right of the vertical fall-line to Raj (as viewed facing the cliff). My anchor, Hugh's tree, was about 25 feet behind me, a little uphill, and to the left of the fall-line. I faced out to look down at Raj. My anchor line was tied to the front of my harness and went around my right side to the anchor tree. I belayed with an ATC, also clipped to the front of my harness. I leaned out a bit to pretension the anchor line. Everything seemed solid, so I yelled down to Raj that he could climb.

Raj fell as he was doing the roof moves, and I discovered instantly that I was unprepared for the magnitude and direction of the force. Although I saw it all in slow motion, everything happened rapidly and simultaneously. The downward force in Raj's belay line buckled my legs. It also "unwrapped" me from the anchor line, torquing me clockwise and destroying any stability that remained. Stretch in the long anchor line sent me over the side. Finally, because I was to the right of the imaginary line between Raj and the anchor, I shot to the left. The net result: I tumbled down and left five or six feet onto a third-class ramp at the top of the climb.

From the first moment, I knew I couldn't stop my fall; but I also knew I was anchored and therefore safe, so I just went with it. I remember thinking that Raj's safety depended on my maintaining his belay; nothing else mattered—I would be OK, but I had to concentrate on that grip. However, as I tumbled across the face and began crashing into rocks and branches, I must have become disoriented—it is all blurry now, but I probably put my hands out in a reflex to protect myself and dropped the rope.

The next thing I knew, I was hanging there a little banged up and I heard the whizzing sound of the rope racing through the ATC. That sound still echoes in my head today. I remember thinking, "If I don't do something now, Raj is going to die." I imagined the end of the rope going through the ATC and Raj sailing through the air, although, in fact, the end of his rope was tied to me.

I instinctively grabbed the rope going into and coming out of the ATC with my bare hands and simultaneously tried to wrap it around my leg. That didn't do much to slow Raj down. A few seconds later— also missing from my mind— I noticed that it was quiet and that the rope had stopped. I wondered, "What stopped it? Me, or Raj hitting something?" Finally I realized that the belay rope was taut and my belay hand was holding it in the arrest position, so I must have made the right moves. I had no idea how long this took or how I did it, but it seemed more practiced reflex than conscious act.

I could see that my hands were shredded, and I was also scared, wondering if my friend had died. I called to Hugh, "Where's Raj, where's Raj?" Finally, I heard Raj's voice nearly a pitch below calling, "Is everything OK?" I looked down at my belay hand, still holding his rope, with blood oozing and chunks of torn skin hanging, and I could not answer him because I did not know. I just sat there, bleeding and holding the rope, for what seemed like 15 minutes.

Meanwhile, Hugh was not sure what had happened. He thought there might have been a problem with the anchor, so he wrapped my line around the tree and was hesitant to let go of it until he knew what was going on. I had not been much help in enlightening him to this point.

Then I saw a guy looking down at me, asking if we needed some help. He was a guide from the Yosemite Mountaineering School and had just finished a nearby route. He was able to scramble down to me, tie off Raj's line with Prusiks, and get me out of the belay, although I do not remember much of it. With a little help I was able to get up to the anchor using my legs and elbows while Hugh belayed me.

I saw that my right hand was covered with giant, fluid-filled blisters, and my left, the belay hand, had much of the skin torn off, with bits hanging loose everywhere. Then came the pain of deep burns. The guide wrapped my hands. An Austrian couple who came by put my hiking boots on, helped me hike down to the car, and drove me to the Yosemite clinic while Hugh and the guide belayed Raj up the pitch.

Later, I found out that Raj had slid 60 or 70 feet by the time I stopped him, and that I probably had 20 feet of rope left. Somehow he managed to stay upright and avoid injury. I am amazed he did not bang into something and at least break his ankle, and I can not imagine what he was thinking. He said later that he did not know if he was going to fall again, so he was trying to find some footholds. He even thought it was a pretty good climb.

The skin on my left hand, where I had gripped the rope, had been completely abraded to the underlying tissue. I needed a few doses of morphine before I felt relief from the pain and the clinic staff could clean up the mess. Once back home, I was amazed to find that my hand was able to heal by itself, without the need for plastic surgery; however, it did require several months of physical therapy to be able to open fully. My harness died in the line of duty. The rope had melted halfway through a leg loop, welding the leg loop to my shorts and burning my leg underneath. (Source: Dan Sokols)

Analysis

Dan deserves lots of credit for stopping Raj under the circumstances, but he could have broken his hand or his skull in the tumble and then been unable to recover Raj's belay.

Some suggestions for stabilizing the belayer. First, avoid taking the force of even a simple top-rope fall directly downward on your harness and legs. The peak force can exceed twice the climber's weight. If there is no other choice, at least belay sitting down. Alternatively, run the line from the climber through a high directional (in some cases, the anchor), so that the force on you is upward (as when belaying a top-roper from below). The harness will be stressed properly, and your own weight, plus friction at the directional, will help counter the force. (Do not forget the strength requirements of the directional.)

Next, if you are not in line with the anchor and the climber, consider these options: a) relocate the anchor, b) build a secondary, directional anchor to oppose the sideways force, or c) establish a directional on the belay line below you to align it with the anchor line. A third point: If stretch in a long anchor line will be a problem, minimize it by distributing the force among two or more strands of rope. Fourth, as in Dan's party of three, let Hugh belay from the original anchor while Dan stands at the edge as a voice relay. (A full discussion of belay forces and solutions requires a textbook.)

Finally, do you and your partners know how to recover from an accident like this? (Source: John Dill, NPS Ranger, Yosemite National Park)

LIGHTNING–POOR POSITION, FAILURE TO TURN BACK, INADEQUATE CLOTHING AND EQUIPMENT
California, Yosemite National Park, Cathedral Peak

On June 25, my brother Andrew Betts (24) and I, Brad Betts (28), along with our friend Richard Meade (26), set out to climb the six-pitch, 5.6 Southeast Buttress of Cathedral Peak (10,940 feet). None of us had done the climb before, and it would be my first significant multi-pitch climb.

We drove up from the Bay Area the night before and camped west of the park, about 50 miles from the trailhead. We had planned to hike the three miles to the base of the route by 8:00 a.m. and be off the summit by 1:00 p.m., to avoid afternoon thunderstorms. However, we awoke at 4:00 a.m., to find that someone—not a bear—had stolen our food, and dealing with that put us two hours behind schedule.

We checked the weather board at the park entrance, but we were too early for the current forecast and the station was still closed. The old forecast called for thunderstorms yesterday but sunny weather today. That was good enough for us, and there was not a cloud in the sky as we started up the climb at 10:00 a.m.

By the end of the second pitch, small, white, puffy clouds were visible in the eastern sky, and by the end of the third pitch, with three more to go, we could see distant rain. Feeling that we were outrunning the storm and knowing that we could quickly descend the backside of the peak, we made a group decision to press on for the top instead of rappelling off. (Andrew was concerned about the ropes hanging up if we retreated, and he later admitted that he was hesitant to leave behind the gear required for safe rappel anchors.)

We raced up the fourth and fifth pitches, hoping to avoid climbing on wet rock, but rain and hail caught us on the sixth—and final—pitch. While I waited to follow Andrew, the hair on the back of my hand stood on end at least twice. It did not take a genius to know that lightning might be close behind, but we were committed to getting up and off by that point.

The wind and rain made communicating with Andrew very difficult. When the ropes to Richard and me came tight, we started up the pitch together in a rush. As we neared the summit, everything around us started to buzz. That was the most terrifying sound I had ever heard!

Not knowing what else to do, Richard and I took shelter under a small overhang of rock, perhaps 20 feet to one side of Andrew's belay. We were all a little below the pinnacle forming the true summit. The crackling buzz continued for over five minutes, and the sky all around us was pitch black. None of us spoke. We remained frozen in place, waiting for the buzzing to stop or to be hit by a bolt. We were scared stiff.

The next thing I remember is a loud crack and being violently slammed into the cliff. I could feel current flowing through my right arm. The buzzing had stopped, but now I could hear Richard moaning. Two other climbers, Bojan Silic and Wolfgang Ertel, had crossed the summit just ahead, and one of them was screaming. Richard and I were shaken but otherwise OK. Then I looked over at Andrew. He was hanging limply from his belay on a steep slab, making a barely audible moaning sound. I screamed at him but he did not respond.

The minutes that followed were chaotic and very dangerous. Andrew had not yet tied us off when the lightning struck, but when Richard yelled at me, "Let's move!" We both scrambled—with no belay—across the wet, 5th class slab to my brother. When I reached him, he was unconscious. His eyes were open but unfocused, he was still moaning, and he smelled of burnt flesh and hair. Richard and I discussed the rigging for 30 seconds or so, and when I turned back to Andrew, his eyes and mouth were closed and he was not making a sound. Worse, he did not seem to be breathing. With my helmet in the way, and the noise from the wind, it was difficult to listen for breathing sounds, but I could not see his chest moving so I started rescue breathing anyway. I was in near disbelief that things could turn so bad so quickly. Perched on that exposed slab, "belayed" only by my unconscious brother, and concentrating on keeping him alive, I could easily have become a second victim. Yet in the rush to help him, this did not occur to me.

The buzzing was gone but the black clouds were still directly overhead. This peak was clearly not the place to be, but to get out we had to move Andrew 30 feet up and around the summit to the descent route. Richard clipped himself to Andrew. Being in a better position near Andrew's face, he also took over rescue breathing. Moving a completely limp 190 pounder was slow going and not gentle. At one point we literally dragged him headfirst down a 20-foot cliff, with his limbs snagging in the cracks. Thankfully, Bojan had come back to help.

For a couple of minutes we had to stop breathing for Andrew to move him. He looked dead, and I felt for a time that I was merely recovering his body. However, perhaps seven minutes after the strike, just as we got him over the top, he began convulsing and screaming. Less than a minute later, he started to regain consciousness, although he was still very confused. I asked him if he knew where he was; he was not sure, but thought probably in British Columbia, his previous home. His confusion gradually subsided over the next couple of hours. He could move now but could not support himself, and he complained of severe neck pain.

Bojan and Wolfgang set up a rappel down steep slabs. Richard tied Andrew tightly to his harness, and Andrew leaned backwards against him while Richard controlled their rappel. They were still on the ropes when the buzzing returned. Bojan and I, at the top, grabbed the ropes and slid down the pitch bare-handed, all four of us loading the anchor at once, but it was a false alarm—no strike this time—and we made one more rappel to easier ground.

Bojan had brought his HAM radio, and about an hour after the strike he finally reached another HAM in Martinez, 150 miles to the west. His contact called the NPS, then relayed back to us that Rangers would come out to look for us. Wolfgang and Bojan went ahead to meet them while we slowly worked our way down the slabs. We were wet and very cold, and Andrew felt like ice. He was weak, vomiting, in pain, and still disoriented. He leaned on one of us at all times and needed constant encouragement to keep moving. I worried that his symptoms indicated some underlying form of shock. We made very slow progress, taking frequent rests.

Bojan ran into the YOSAR crew and guided them to us around 6:00 p.m., three-and-a-half hours after the strike. Andrew was unable to continue on foot. Because of his neck pain, YOSAR immobilized him in a litter, then they wheeled him out to the road while Richard and I walked. A waiting ambulance took Andrew and me to the hospital at Mammoth Lakes. Richard, Bojan, and Wolfgang had all been stunned momentarily by the bolt, but the dice had come up in their favor; they were released at the trailhead with only a few minor injuries and a story to tell.

At the hospital, Andrew and I were treated for minor burns and dehydration. His spine was OK, but he was groggy and extremely weak for 24 hours. We were released after two days, but two weeks later Andrew developed severe pain and weakness in his right shoulder and back. He had a condition known as "winging scapula," a result of damage to the long thoracic nerve. The nerve is expected to regenerate within a year, as nerves outside the spinal column do regrow, albeit slowly.

Analysis

I (Andrew) was the instigator of this trip, the most experienced member, and the de facto leader, so the responsibility for decisions was mine. In my opinion, the accident was a direct result of insufficient preparation in at least three ways: (1) We did not have the current weather forecast. Instead, we relied on a day-old report, unaware of predicted lightning in the high country. Up-to-date information would have allowed us to better plan the day, perhaps choosing shorter routes close to the road instead of tackling a remote, multi-pitch route. In retrospect, a weather radio or a visit to the Ranger Station would have been wise. (2) We lacked proper gear for alpine conditions. Brad and I wore cotton clothing, affectionately referred to as "death cloth" by the YOSAR crew. It is colder than synthetics when wet, and slower to dry. Furthermore, we had no rain gear and no way to start a fire. In our condition, we faced serious hypothermia if we had had had to bivouac at 10,000 feet that night. We had a single headlamp, but no other signaling devices, so we were very fortunate that Bojan had his HAM radio. (3) Finally, and most importantly, we did not stick to our safety plan. Once behind schedule, we just tried to catch up. In fact, we had no explicit plan for bailing once the climb began. Without criteria for retreat—dark clouds on the horizon, etc.—we kept moving up until fleeing in either direction was equally risky.

In the final analysis, we got into trouble because we raced for the summit instead of retreating. All other considerations—forecasts, rain jackets—were secondary. Preparation is important, but no substitute for intelligent analysis of the developing conditions.

Brad's and Richard's first aid training may have saved my life. Brad was not sure if I had actually stopped breathing, so he played it safe. If there is any uncertainty, do not waste time—properly done, assisted breathing will not hurt your patient.

I would like to sincerely thank Bojan and Wolfgang for remaining at the summit to help in spite of the obvious danger of staying. Without their aid things would have been a whole lot uglier. My eternal thanks!

Months later, I still remember very little about the strike. Oddly, I think that makes me the lucky one. The true victims are the people who do remember: Brad and Richard, worrying if I would survive the day; my family, receiving the late-night call; my girlfriend, upon whom I placed tremendous demands during my recovery. As we take risks with our own lives, we risk a part of the lives of all those who love and care for us. I still climb, but I do so with a new and profound respect for everyone emotionally tied to the rope with me. (Source: Andrew and Brad Betts, and John Dill, NPS Ranger, Yosemite National Park)

(Editor's Note: Mother Nature chose her targets with a sense of humor: Four are electrical engineers and one is a computer science pro.)

FALLING ROCK— DISLODGED, NO HARD HAT, POOR POSITION
California, Yosemite Valley, Sentinel Rock

On June 27, Jim Corpus (44) and Mike Penner (45) climbed the Steck-Salathe route (15 pitches, 5.9) on Sentinel Rock. They summited at sunset, took a break, and started looking for the 3rd class descent gully after dark. Despite having headlamps, they had trouble finding their way and wound up descending slabs on the south side of the gully, where they encountered lots of loose rocks.

About midnight, halfway down the slabs, with Jim 100-150 feet ahead of and below Mike, Mike's foot dislodged a 5-10 pound rock. He yelled, "Rock!" and listened as it bounced down the face, and then called for Jim, but got no response. He scrambled down the slab and found only a headlamp where Jim should have been. Beyond the lamp, patches of blood led another 150 feet downhill to where Jim lay, unconscious and bleeding from his scalp. He was just two feet short of a 40-foot cliff that probably would have finished him off.

Mike: "After several minutes Jim started mumbling, and his level of consciousness improved slowly but considerably through the night. Immediately after the accident he couldn't process what had happened, asking the same questions over and over: 'Where are we? What happened? Is this real? Got any water?'

"I didn't apply pressure to Jim's wound because touching it was intensely painful to him. After awhile I decided that he probably wasn't bleeding severely, despite the initial amount of blood. I was sure he'd suffered a severe concussion, possibly a skull fracture, and he was in shock. I got him into his jacket, put my jacket over his legs and a rope underneath him and made him as comfortable as possible without moving him much.

"I couldn't find anchors and I wanted to keep him from rolling off the ledge we were on, so I just sat next to him all night holding him in place. I wasn't sure of the way out, anyway, and the light from my headlamp didn't allow me to see a safe way down.

"As it began to get light, I was able to improvise some anchors and tie him in. By this time he was more lucid and really wanted to get to a more comfortable position, but I didn't want him to. When dawn arrived I could see where we were and where we were supposed to be and took off for help."

Mike reached his vehicle—and his cell phone—at about 0830 and called the NPS. While a ground team scrambled up the descent route, a helicopter from Naval Air Station Lemoore searched from the air; the crew spotted Jim and rappelled two Rangers and a Navy crewman to him. He was alert by this time, though still complaining of dizziness. They immobilized him as a precaution against spinal injury, and the helicopter hoisted him out shortly after 1100.

X-rays at the Yosemite clinic showed no fractures. Because of his head injury, he was helicoptered to Doctors Medical Center in Modesto for further tests, but was later released, with only a severe scalp laceration and minor cuts and bruises.

Analysis

Jim and Mike are both very experienced climbers. They were not far off route, but even the correct way down that gully is a potential bowling alley. When you cannot see the rocks coming at you and your ability to dodge them is restricted, it is usually best to stick close together.

Mike: "I know descending can be more dangerous than ascending, and I've always been extremely careful with rappels. I never expected such an accident on a walk-down, but loose rock is a danger wherever you find it.

"We didn't have helmets. The rock that hit Jim might have knocked him out or off his feet even if he'd been wearing one, but a helmet surely would have lessened the damage and the risks.

"In retrospect, we should have just bivouacked on the summit. We'd been climbing all day without much water and ran dry before the top. It was a pleasant night and there are some nice sandy spots there, but we were thirsty and were lured downward by the crashing of Sentinel Creek. Ironically, the medics did not allow Jim even one sip of water until he was cleared of internal injuries in Modesto the next afternoon!

"My advice for Sentinel climbers: If you top out at sundown, have a seat. Don't lose the route on the walk-down, and keep your helmet on till you hit the Four-Mile Trail.

"Months after the accident, three thoughts stand out: First, it's remarkable

how lucky we were. Aside from the fact that the rock or the tumble down the slab didn't kill him, it's a miracle that Jim stopped short of that big drop. Second, we were lucky to be in Yosemite, because the job the NPS and the Navy did was truly impressive. Finally, the time that passed between dislodging the rock and finding Jim alive was only a minute or two, but it was the most horrifying moment of my life." (Source: John Dill, NPS Ranger, Yosemite National Park)
(Editor's Note: For more about rockfall, see CA incidents on 4/24 and 8/12 in this issue of ANAM.)

OFF ROUTE–FALL ON ROCK, INADEQUATE EQUIPMENT AND PROTECTION
California, Yosemite Valley, Royal Arches
Welsh climbers Dan McDonald (20) and Peris Roberts (20) started climbing Royal Arches (17 pitches, 5.9) at 1130 on August 1. The route was well within their abilities, and they finished it with no problems, reaching the patch of woods at the end of the last regular pitch at about 1830.

While looking for the 3rd class exit to the rim—a scramble up and left, then a few easy moves through summit overhangs, their attention was drawn to an obvious path descending to the left. They followed it until it dead ended on the cliff face at the base of a slab that appeared to lead to the top. They decided to try the slab, so Peris put Dan on belay. Dan was expecting 3rd class and this looked easy, so he did not bother taking protection along or changing back into his climbing shoes.

He climbed 10-15 feet of loose 5.6-5.7—harder than he had expected, then he fell when either a hold broke off or his feet slipped. He grabbed a two inch diameter bush that he had used climbing up, but it came out by the roots. He took a sliding fall of about 20 feet, stopping in some tree branches ten feet below Peris. He realized right away that he had dislocated his shoulder, but nothing else seemed to be injured. He was secure where he had landed, so Peris took him off belay, scrambled down to him, and tried, unsuccessfully, to get his shoulder back into place. It was now about 1930, and an hour of daylight remained.

Dan was able to belay, so Peris took over the lead. He climbed another ramp up and left, toward the falls from Royal Arches Creek, but this was also harder than 3rd class. He did not think Dan would be able to follow, so he turned back. They considered having Peris solo up the ramp he had just explored and go for help, but they were almost out of daylight. They chose, instead, to stick together, stay where they were, and signal for help.

They tried shouting and whistle blasts in groups of three, with no luck. Finally, after several hours, they managed to alert someone on the Valley floor by using their lone flashlight and the flash on their camera. At midnight, Rangers contacted them with a loudspeaker from the base of the cliff.

Two NPS rescue team members started up the Royal Arches route at 0045 on August 2 and reached Dan and Peris an hour and a half later. They helped Dan up the correct Class 3 route to the rim and made camp. In the morning he was flown out by the park helicopter, and his shoulder dislocation was reduced at the Yosemite clinic.

Analysis

Dan feels he could have finished the pitch if he had taken his gear; instead, he was essentially climbing unroped—a pretty common scenario behind climbing accidents in the park. With the climb "over," expecting 3rd class, and close to dark, the failure to recognize changing circumstances (known as "situational awareness") can probably take credit for another victim. In addition, a little more exploration before committing to that slab would have uncovered the normal 3rd class exit indicated in the guidebook.

Dan and Peris had a spare rope, but no matches or extra clothes, and only one light. We strongly recommend one headlamp per person on any long route—it is hard to share a Mini-Mag at opposite ends of the rope. We also recommend training as a Wilderness First Responder. Among other skills, it will improve your ability to deal with dislocations, especially when no rescue team is waiting to bail you out. (Source: John Dill, NPS Ranger, Yosemite National Park)

FALL ON ROCK
California, Yosemite Valley, Half Dome

On August 4 about 0800, two climbers reported to Ranger Steve Yu that one member of their party of five Koreans had broken his right leg in a fall the previous day on the Regular Northwest Face (VI 5.9 A2) of Half Dome. They had managed to move the injured climber, Young-Jin Kim (24), to the base of pitch 9. Then the two reporting climbers had rappelled off to get help, leaving Kim in the care of the other members of the team. Apparently the fracture was open and had bled heavily for a time. (None of the climbers spoke English, but Steve solved the problem by calling his father, who is fluent in Korean, at his home in Wisconsin.)

Steve became the incident commander. He paged out the SAR team for a rope rescue from the summit and requested H551, the park A-Star helicopter. He also requested Rescue Six, the UH-1N Huey helicopter from Naval Air Station Lemoore, in case a hoist from the cliff face were required. (The face is a bit less than vertical on this part of the route.)

We flew one team member to the summit—to keep hikers from dropping cameras and day-packs onto the helicopters below—then Ranger Keith Lober and I flew a recon of the cliff face with H551. Pilot Dana Morris and crew chief Karen Kufta found they could hover directly over a two-foot wide sloping ramp that was about 25 feet below the climbers. We had about 15 feet of tip-to-cliff rotor clearance as a safety margin, so we decided to do the operation entirely by air, leaving the ground team in reserve. Clouds were building over Half Dome, so the faster we got this done, the less likely we would be out there in a lightning storm.

Keith rappelled first with a rack of hardware, a hand drill, ropes and medical gear. The rock was rotten where he landed but he was able to get in two quick pitons and a cam. Then I rappelled with the litter.

The Koreans lowered their one remaining rope to us (their friends having rappelled with the other two). We did not know what sort of anchor they had, so we declined their offer, and Keith led the short section up to them with our own gear. When he got there he found all three climbers attached to the only available protection, a single ⅜-inch bolt. Keith backed it up with a couple of ¼-inch buttonheads and fixed his line for me, while I assembled the litter where we had landed.

Kim was basically OK except for his ankle. His shoe was still on his foot, and blood soaked, but the bleeding had stopped hours ago. Our stance was cramped and the shoe stabilized Kim's injury fairly well, so, after checking his spine, we packaged him in the litter, deferring a complete assessment to the medics waiting in the Valley.

Winds remained calm, and H551 had no problem short-hauling Kim from our position. He was at the clinic by about 1230. An open tib/fib fracture at the ankle was confirmed, and he was flown by the Air-Med helicopter to Doctors Medical Center in Modesto for orthopedic surgery.

Meanwhile, Rescue Six made two flights to hoist out the four of us remaining on the wall. With its larger rotor diameter, the Huey had to stand about 20 feet further out than our A-Star. They lowered a crew member, who dangled in space in front of us. We threw him a line and hauled him over to the ledge so that he could supervise the hookups.

Analysis
From looking at the scene and gesturing with the Koreans, I think that Kim was leading a 5.9 crack on pitch 10. He was hit by a sudden hail storm that coated the rock with ice, which is common on Half Dome, even in August. I do not know if he considered retreating to the belay or clipping to a piece until conditions improved, but either would have been a wise choice. Instead he kept climbing, took a fall of about ten feet, and his foot struck something on the way down. (Source Mike Nash, NPS Ranger, Yosemite National Park)

FALL ON ROCK, NO HARD HAT
California, Yosemite National Park, Tuolumne Meadows
On August 12, Chris Weeldreyer (36) was leading the first pitch (5.9+) of Needle Spoon, a face climb on Pywiack Dome in Tuolumne Meadows, belayed by Henry Cutler. Near the end of the pitch, 5-10 feet above his last protection (a bolt), his feet slipped and he fell over backward, striking his head. He fell 10-20 feet and stopped, unconscious and hanging upside down with blood running down the rock from a scalp laceration. He woke up about a minute later and was able to right himself. Henry lowered him to the belay and applied a pressure dressing to the wound. Chris only remembers falling, then waking up at the belay with a bloody head.

Chris was able to make the rappel down 3rd class terrain and walk out a few hundred yards to the road. By this time he was fully alert, but the NPS medics were concerned about possible skull and neck fractures. Chris was given oxygen and an IV, immobilized on a backboard, and flown to Mammoth Lakes Hospital for X-rays. He was released that evening, with no fractures.

Analysis

We do not know the level of experience of these climbers. We do know that climbers here often choose not to wear helmets. Sometimes they get away with it. (Source: John Dill, NPS Ranger, Yosemite National Park, and Jed Williamson)

FALLING ROCK— DISLODGED BY DAY-PACK, POOR POSITION
California, Yosemite Valley, Cathedral Rocks

On August 12, Sarah Sand (59) and eight friends started up the Gunsight, the class 4-5 gully between Middle and Lower Cathedral Rocks. David (58), the leader, had been bringing friends on this climb for several years. As usual, he had given the beginners, including Sarah, at least one day of instruction at a local climbing area to get them competent at basic skills.

By 1130 they had scrambled up the 2nd and 3rd class scree slope to the base of the first roped pitch, a 70-foot buttress blocking the gully. The Gunsight is full of loose rock, so at this point, as was his habit, David talked about rockfall hazards and made sure they all had their helmets on.

The group waited at the base of the pitch while David climbed. At the top he set down his day pack while he established an anchor. The rock surface was solid, with just a few chunks of granite scattered about, but the pack brushed a grapefruit-sized piece and sent it rolling toward the edge.

David lunged after the rock, but he knew it was too late. He yelled "Rock! Rock!" hoping the group would hug the cliff as he had stressed in his talk. Everybody below yelled "Rock!" and ran for cover. Sarah was standing on a ledge along one wall of the gully, 30 feet away from the rock's fall-line. She started to move but thought better of it and crouched down where she was, covering her head.

The rock bounced outward, striking her in the back, on the lower left ribs. There was instant pain in her side. In a few minutes it was clear that this was not a blow she was going to recover from on the spot, nor would she be able to walk out, so two members of the group went for help while the rest tried to make her comfortable. After half an hour, Sarah's stomach started burning. She thought it was just nerves, or maybe heartburn, so she took a couple of Tums.

The reporting party drove up to the NPS SAR Office at 1415, about two-0and-a-half hours after the accident. I left for the scene 15 minutes later with two other team members. When we arrived, at 1515, Sarah was lying on her back on a sloping ledge, kept from sliding down the gully by her friends. She was fully alert and outwardly calm, even displaying a sense of humor. There was nothing in her personality that might raise the alarm. Her vital signs were normal for her, she could breath without difficulty, and her lungs were clear.

There was pain where the rock had hit her and the site was only bruised, with no significant deformity. It hurt to move and she could feel a "crunchy" sensation suggestive of broken ribs.

The "heartburn" under her diaphragm increased when we pressed gently on her abdomen. Palpating the left upper abdominal quadrant caused "muscle" pain in that area and also down her left arm. Deep breathing caused pain in her lower chest and down her arm. (With no trauma besides the rock's impact, the arm pain was probably "referred" pain, a frequent symptom of internal bleeding.) There was no abdominal rigidity or guarding.

Her symptoms did not seem to have worsened much over time except for an increase in "heartburn" along her sides, but all of these observations were signs of potentially serious internal bleeding, and the mechanism of injury suggested damage to her internal organs.

We gave Sarah oxygen and IV fluids, and packaged her in a litter. Because of the mechanism of injury and our physical exam, we were able to rule out the need to immobilize her spine, making packaging faster and more comfortable for her. The oxygen and IV seemed to ease the pain, but if she did have serious internal bleeding, she would need surgery as soon as possible. The most important field treatments were gentle handling and a fast rescue.

We had hoped to evacuate Sarah by helicopter short-haul, but shifting winds aloft made the tight quarters in the gully too dangerous. As other team members arrived, they began rigging belays, and with the help of a guiding line, we worked our way down the gully, lowering the litter over short drops and negotiating very loose terrain. When the litter briefly dipped footward over a steep section, Sarah fainted until she leveled out again—a strong indication of blood loss.

We reached the road at about 2000, eight hours after the accident. Sarah went by ambulance, then by helicopter to Doctors Medical Center in Modesto. She was admitted as a "code blue"—a patient in a life-or-death situation—and taken to surgery. The hospital staff estimated that by the time she arrived, she had lost a third of her blood to internal bleeding.

Sarah had seven broken ribs, a damaged kidney, and a ruptured spleen—the primary source of bleeding—as well as other complications that arose during her recovery. The spleen was removed and over the next two months she was in and out of the hospital several times. She returned to work and normal exercise.

Analysis

David: "I've been climbing and watching my step for 40 years. But when I put that pack down, I just wasn't careful enough. I've relived it in my mind 100,000 times."

Almost every climber has caused rockfall. Most of us were simply lucky that the trajectory did not include our partner. David is right—you simply cannot let down your guard.

David had suggested to his friends that they avoid falling rock by flattening themselves against the cliff. That is often the right move, but if you have time, first look up to judge the rock's path. Maybe what you see will suggest a better response, realizing, of course, that rocks can take crazy bounces. Also, avoid belaying or standing around under the climber if you do not need to be there. If you cannot keep everyone out of the way, take a small group in the first place. This had been David's practice in the past and will be in the future. He also made the point that the tendency of a large group of friends to socialize may distract them from the business at hand. Finally, this case is a good reminder that blunt trauma often results in a hidden but potentially fatal injury. (Source: John Dill, NPS Ranger, Yosemite National Park)

(Editor's Note: The lengthy description of patient assessment and care was left in to demonstrate what the quality of emergency care in the wilderness should look like.)

FALL ON ROCK, PROTECTION PULLED OUT, PLACED INADEQUATE PROTECTION, NO HARD HAT
California, Yosemite Valley, Reed's Pinnacle

On September 23, Aram Marks (21) was leading Stone Groove, a one-pitch 5.10b crack at Reed's Pinnacle. Tricia (29) was belaying at the base. Aram placed a piece about 10 feet up, followed by a TCU at about 15 feet. He continued climbing until his feet were 7-10 feet above the TCU, then he stopped to place another piece.

He tried to place a .75 Camalot but dropped it. He got nervous, knowing that the TCU below was over-cammed and shallow. He was balanced on one foot and stretched out, trying to put in a nut, when he fell. The TCU pulled out, making a ground fall inevitable, but the fall was partially broken when he glanced off his belayer. Although knocked out, he regained consciousness after about two minutes.

Tricia and two nearby climbers kept him from moving, stabilized his head, and checked his pulse and breathing. Two others called 911 and the NPS arrived about 45 minutes later. Aram was awake but still showing signs of a concussion, e.g., asking the same questions repeatedly. The team administered oxygen and an IV, immobilized his spine, and carried him down to the road. The Yosemite clinic ambulance took him directly to the NPS heli-base at Crane Flat, from where he was flown to Doctors Medical Center in Modesto.

Aram had received a mild concussion (he still does not remember the fall), a head laceration requiring several staples, and various abrasions, but he avoided more serious injuries. Tricia, the fall-breaker, got away with a bruised knee and a chipped bone in her hand.

Analysis

The stances on Stone Groove are a bit tricky, but the placements are solid. You should be able to eliminate a ground-fall if you make protection your priority. On any route, if marginal pieces expose you to a risky fall, do not just look above for the next placement. Consider placing a piece at waist level or lower, as insurance. Aram was not wearing a helmet. He was lucky, because colliding with Tricia diverted him from several sharp rocks in the landing zone. (Source: John Dill, NPS Ranger, Yosemite)

INCOMPLETE TIE-IN, FALL ON ROCK
California, The Needles, Sorcerer Needle

On September 4, two climbers were on Thin Ice (5.10b) at the Needles, an easy route for their abilities, after earlier climbing two short, multi-pitch routes, Igor Unchained (5.9) and Airy Interlude (5.10a). It was 1530, the route was in shade with a mild breeze, and both climbers were wearing jackets. Patrick Savageau (20) belayed leader Dan DeLange of Colorado on the first pitch, then followed.

Savageau had tied in after his partner led the pitch, then followed, and due to the jacket, his partner could not see his knot. He clipped into the anchor with a sling clipped to the loop of rope created by the (incomplete) knot. At 1545, after switching the rack to lead the second pitch, Savageau leaned back to scope out the pitch, and immediately fell, as the figure eight knot had not been finished. He fell 250 feet to his death. If he had weighted the rope at any point while following the first pitch, he would have fallen. He was not wearing a helmet, but it would have made no difference. Three climbers at the base of Igor Unchained, 100 yards away, also witnessed the accident, and immediately attempted to come to his assistance, but found him dead of massive injuries.

Analysis

Dan DeLange had 20 years of climbing experience. Patrick Savageau had only been climbing three years, yet had on-sighted 5.12 crack. A partner commented, "Pat was one of a few. He was a major go-for-it in a way that I've seen only a few times in my 20+ years of climbing. Last year he was 19 and had been climbing only a season or two. When we'd head to the Valley, he'd always want to do the hard cracks. The only problem was that he'd done most that were easily accessible. We rapped down to Tales of Power [5.12b] where he made an impressive ascent, just a hang or two. He had the hardest trouble with the chimney at the top. On the next day we did Uprising on the Rostrum. Pat ran out of gear at the top and had to lead the last 20 feet of 5.11+ without pro. I was impressed. Then we went over and jumped on the Cosmic Debris TR (5.13b). With just a hang or two he was grabbing the top slings. Strong and determined, that's how I'll remember Pat."

There is a simple four-point check that is becoming routine for many climbers: Doubled-back, rope through harness correctly, figure 8 correct, double-fisherman back-up knot correct. And for the belayer: doubled-back, belay 'biner through harness correctly, 'biner locked, rope threaded correctly. Such checks should always be done by all partners on each other, regardless of experience. (Source: Greg Barnes, who witnessed the accident)

FALL ON SNOW, CLIMBING UNROPED, PLACED NO PROTECTION
California, Mount Shasta, Hotlum/Bolam Ridge

Leaving their high camp in the early morning of September 23, Dave Woods and David Wicken (36) began the 40-degree climb of the Hotlum/Bolam Ridge. Woods fell twice during the ascent, but was able to self-arrest. Skirting the western crevasses and bergschrund of the Hotlum Glacier, they reached 12,000 feet by 0500. Concerned with the water ice and hard snow on the route, they moved toward some rocks to rest. Wieken lost his balance and fell. Unable to self-arrest on the hard snow and water ice patches, he continued to fall.

Dave Woods descended, looking for his partner. He encountered a guided trip who helped him search. Shasta Mountain Guides found Wieken's helmet, then lower down at 11,000 feet found Wieken. He was unconscious and unresponsive, showing obvious head and spinal injuries.

Siskiyou County SAR and USFS rangers were called by cell phone. Wieken was short-hauled by the Highway Patrol helicopter down to 8,500 feet, then the Mercy Air helicopter flew him straight to Mercy Hospital. He died from his injuries one week later.

Analysis

The Hotlum/Bolam Ridge is non-technical during most of the climbing season. However, it becomes more difficult and hazardous each season by August or September with the formation of hard snow and water ice. Climbers have frequently been drawn to the rocks when they become uncomfortable on the route. Unfortunately, this is the first place water ice forms. Although few people use ropes or protection on this route during the main climbing season, roping up *and* using protection may be a good idea in the late season.

Wieken was wearing a helmet, but as it came off during the fall, it may have been loosely fastened. (Source: Eric White and Matt Hill, USFS Climbing Rangers)

(Editor's Note: Two other climbers fell on this route a week later, one suffering a broken leg. A total of 33 accidents were reported from Mount Shasta this year, of which 17 are "eligible" for the data—even though several of them involved rank beginners who were either stranded [total of 12 people] or who lost it glissading [seven]. The rangers have a website that reports conditions and summarizes incidents: www.r5.fs.fed.us/shastatrinity/mtshasta/accident.htm)

NEARLY STRANDED—RIGGING PROBLEMS, DARKNESS, FATIGUE
California, Yosemite Valley, Lost Arrow Tip

Sasha Binford and I, Charles Zilm (32), set out to climb the Lost Arrow Tip (three pitches, 5.8 A2) on October 6. We had hoped to be off by early afternoon, but when we got to the climb at 8:00 a.m. there were already two parties ahead of us rappelling into the notch. We were looking at a long day, but I still figured we would be off before sunset. It warmed up quickly in the sun, but I threw a warm shirt and pile jacket into Sasha's pack anyway. I had climbed the Tip four years ago, finishing in the dark, and remembered being really cold.

The Arrow Tip is a pinnacle that attaches to the main wall 250 feet below the rim of the Valley and rises to a finger-tip summit a little below the rim. The climb starts in the notch where the Arrow joins the wall; to get there we made one long rappel from the rim on two single lines tied together. Then we waited an hour or two for the party ahead of us to clear the first pitch. I led the climb on a third rope. I dragged the bottom end of the rappel lines with me, leaving the other end fixed to the anchor tree on the rim. The two rappel ropes would become a Tyrolean traverse from the top of the Arrow back to the rim, a gap of about 75 feet plus the climb up to the anchor.

The climb went fine, and I reached the top about an hour before dark, as the party ahead crossed to the rim and pulled their lines. I pulled most of the slack out of our rappel line and tied it off, giving us one Tyrolean line across the gap. When Sasha finished cleaning the pitch, I put her on belay with our lead rope; she clipped a locking carabiner over the Tyrolean line, to hang from while she traversed, and clipped the end of the second rappel line to her harness, to take it across. I lowered her out until she had descended to the low point in the traverse, then she jugged up the other side to the rim.

Sasha tied off the end of the second rope, and I rigged the ropes through the anchor on the summit so that we could pull them after I got across. It was too dark to see anything clearly now. I had not brought a headlamp, so I had to double- and triple-check everything. The knot joining the two ropes was probably two-thirds of the way across the gap, although I could not see it in the gloom.

Four years ago I had crossed the Tyrolean by using a single Prusik around both lines to let myself down to the low point; it was not very efficient, but it had worked. (*Ed. Note: Two Prusiks would be better.*) I had read somewhere about rappelling the descending side and thought this might be more efficient, so this time I rigged both lines through my ATC. Like Sasha, I clipped a second locking carabiner from my harness to the ropes, to support myself.

Rappelling was easy as long as there was no tension in the ropes below me, but as the lines to the rim became snug from my weight, the friction in the ATC brought me to a halt. I was still short of the low point. I started pulling myself along with my ascenders, but the friction limited me to an inch or so at a time. It was exhausting and I had to stop many times to rest. I found that I could not unclip the ATC and take it off the ropes. I thought of going back to the summit and starting over without it, but it would be cold and windy up there and I could not see to re-rig. Besides, I thought it would be a waste of time—I should be able to resolve any problems right here, and it would take longer to go back up than to keep going.

I knew that I could remove the ATC when the tension diminished as I started up the other side. I still could not see the knot, and I knew I would not be able to pass it with the ATC still on the ropes. I hoped it was close enough to the wall to relieve the tension, but when I reached the knot after at least an hour, the ropes were still too tight. In hindsight, I wonder why I was so stubborn, but I still did not want to spend the time to go back.

By this time it was cold and blowing pretty hard, and I was stuck there in shorts and a T-shirt. Thinking I would be across in no time, I had forgotten to take my clothes from Sasha's pack. She had brought along a pair of FRS (family band) radios so I was able to ask her to send down my shirt and headlamp. I was so cold I was slurring my words, and without the radios we could not have heard each other against the wind.

The shirt and headlamp got stuck on the rope several times, finally just out of reach on the other side of the knot, but I was able to shake the ropes enough to get them to me. The tips of my fingers were now so numb from the cold that I was afraid I would drop my shirt. My speech became so slurred that it was an effort to say anything to Sasha. There was chatter on the radio from the Valley, and I was upset that they would talk when they knew we were using it. One guy was trying to pick up girls on our channel. The contrast between his situation and mine annoyed me.

All this time I had been trying various ways to free my ATC; e.g., by rotating the nose of the carabiner up and trying to roll the ropes out. But there was too much tension in the line and I was too tired.

I told Sasha a couple of times, "I don't know what to do." Someone in the Valley heard this and asked if they should contact Search and Rescue. I did not answer. I did not want to be rescued off a climb—but Sasha answered, "Yes, contact Search and Rescue." SAR was on the radio quickly, asking us questions about my situation and making suggestions. I was pretty punchy by then and probably did not answer very intelligently. I was getting colder so I had Sasha send down another layer of clothes.

Then the Rangers turned two spotlights on me. I felt like the high-wire act for the evening, imagining crowds gathering in the village below to watch the idiot die above them.

I lost radio contact with everyone—Sasha, the Park Service, and the guy picking up girls. I thought the batteries had died, but the radio worked fine afterward so I must have just bumped the volume knob. I was too punchy or distracted to figure it out.

Now both hands were numb and my arm muscles cramped. The wind blew very hard and I knew I could not stay there in those conditions. I finally decided to go back to the Arrow summit and try again. I put one ascender on each line, worrying that, since the ropes were rigged through the anchor on the Arrow, the ascenders would see-saw. But there was enough friction in the system that I could push both simultaneously. Jugging back was much easier than going toward the main wall. I was only partway back when I noticed that the ATC was now loose. I de-rigged it, so relieved.

I down-climbed with my ascenders, holding both ropes together above them to keep the see-sawing under control. Prusiks around both ropes were an option but too much trouble at the time, being so close to the low point. When I got there I turned the ascenders around and climbed to the rim. My fingers were almost useless—I could not feel the ascenders and it was a challenge to work the cams. I found out later that, when the NPS learned I had solved my problem, they turned around their SAR team, halfway up the trail to the Arrow.

I thought I had been on the line for an hour or two, but Sasha stunned me—six hours! I was pretty hard on myself for a while. My fingers, numb for three weeks, reminded me. Would anyone want to do a serious climb with me again? But everyone was very supportive. I screwed up big, but it was an incredibly valuable learning experience.

Analysis

How many things can you find wrong with my picture? I had not actually practiced my "new" way of starting the Tyrolean, because I had done the climb previously, and I also had not thought through the possible problems—not that I could anticipate them all, anyway. They say that in a crisis you revert to your training, and my training did not include this predicament. When I got out there, I could not see solutions that someone standing next to me might have spotted immediately.

Also, I had assumed I would be off before it got dark and cold. With my headlamp, I might have retreated to the Arrow immediately. I became dependent on Sasha, sitting on the rim with headlamp and clothing, and dependent on the radios that she had thought to bring. What if she had not brought them? What if the clothing and headlamp had become stuck on the line, out of reach? Nevertheless, radios and headlamp should not be a substitute for experience.

Park Service comments: It may seem obvious now, but if you decide to rappel the descending portion of the Tyrolean lines, de-rig your brake before the ropes below you become tight. Second, if you do need to escape from this type of brake while the rope is under tension, remember that you can take your weight off the carabiner, but not off the rope, as the tension continues to trap the carabiner against the brake, making it extremely difficult to unclip, as Charles found out. However, the link between the carabiner and the harness is *not* under tension, so unclipping from the belay loop on your harness is a five-second, one-handed manoeuver. But Charles had rigged the carabiner around his leg loops, his waist belt, and a back-up webbing swami, thus making a complicated jumble of stuff to manipulate with numb fingers while hanging there in the dark. By the time he got his headlamp, he was too tired to deal with it.

Regardless of the technique you choose for crossing, you can eliminate the need to pass the knot by just positioning it at the anchor you start from, and have the first person across adjust the slack in both lines as needed. One final comment: This report is not an instruction text on how to rig or cross a horizontal line. (Source: Charles Zilm and John Dill, NPS Ranger, Yosemite National Park)

FALL ON ROCK, INADEQUATE ANCHOR SYSTEM
California, Yosemite Valley, Washington Column

On December 3, Andrew Morrison died when he fell several hundred feet from the South Face of Washington Column (Grade V, 11 pitches, 5.10a A2) in Yosemite Valley. On December 1, they climbed the three pitches to Dinner Ledge and slept on the ledge at the top of pitch 1. They admitted to being awed by the exposure. The climb starts from 3rd class ledges, yielding a few hundred feet of exposure on the first pitch—but they were all enthusiastic, enjoying the climb, and they felt the whole team was climbing competently and safely. Andy had done well leading the second pitch.

On December 2, they hauled their gear to Dinner Ledge, where they planned to bivy until they finished the route. They had lots of trouble with the haulbags snagging on the way up, and they had worked hard getting them free. Pitch 4, the Kor Roof, was Andy's lead, but he was tired from dealing with the bags, so Matt led and Nick followed. It was dark by the time they finished the pitch.

On the third, Andy started up the ropes to lead pitch 5, but had to go to the bathroom, so he returned to Dinner Ledge after jugging halfway. He was still feeling tired, so Matt took the lead with Nick belaying. Andy started up again but then changed his mind. He also mentioned that he had found his ascenders inefficient the first time up, so he had switched to Prusiks.

After a discussion with Matt, Andy decided he would take two ropes and go down to the Valley to get Craig, another member of their group who was hoping to join them. Andy said he planned to rappel pitch 3, pull his rappel ropes, fix one rope as he descended pitch 2, and fix the other on pitch 1. This way, he and Craig would have to re-lead only pitch 3 to rejoin the team. Andy started down from Dinner Ledge and was soon out of sight, while Matt and Nick began pitch 5.

About an hour later Andy called up, "My ropes are stuck." Nick (belaying Matt) replied, "Do you have both ends of the ropes?" Andy: "Yes." Nick: "Can you tie a Prusik around both ropes, then climb up and free them?" Andy: "Oh, yeah," with an apologetic tone, as if realizing he should have thought of that on his own. Nick reinforced the point about the Prusik hitch needing to be around both ropes, and asked for confirmation that Andy understood. Andy seemed frustrated, but not unusually so for someone dealing with the hassles of a wall climb.

Perhaps 45-60 minutes later (approximately 1330), Matt and Nick heard the sound of rocks falling. Matt looked down and saw Andy fall into view, accompanied by one or two watermelon-size rocks. Matt knew immediately that the fall would be fatal. He was able to alert hikers on the ground, and by the time he and Nick had rappelled to Dinner Ledge they could see emergency vehicles on the bicycle path below. Too upset to continue down, they stopped for the night and descended in the morning.

Analysis

Andrew (28), Mathew Ryan (30) and Nicholas Thain (28) were on their first trip to the park, under the sponsorship of the Australian Army Alpine Association. They were competent free climbers with several years experience, but had climbed only a few aid pitches and no big walls. Hoping to improve their wall skills, they had selected the South Face as a good "starter" route. They were well equipped with gear and intended to take several relaxed days, bivouacking on the wall.

The NPS team found that both of Andy's ropes had fallen with him—a 50-meter dynamic and a 46-meter static. The ropes were tied together as if for a rappel. An overhand knot was tied in the free end of the 50-meter rope, similar to a "stopper" knot intended to prevent a rappeller from going off the end of the rope. The free end of the 46-meter rope was unknotted. Andy may have untied a stopper knot in that rope to prevent it from jamming in the rappel anchor when he pulled his ropes down after a rappel.

The accident probably occurred on pitch 3, for the following reasons: (1) The ropes appear to have been rigged for a doubled-rope rappel, and pitch 3 is the only one Andy intended to descend that way. (2) A crack near the top of pitch 3 is well known among locals for jamming rappel ropes, which pitch 2 does not do. (3) It is unlikely that he would have left his ascenders and etriers at the anchor as he descended pitch 2.

Andy's rigging suggests that he was trying to put full body-weight on the 50-meter rope to pull the jammed rope free. Given his position on the rope and the length of pitch 3, he was probably at or near the anchor at the bottom of the pitch, about where he would be if he were pulling his ropes.

Did the falling rocks somehow cause his fall? There is no direct evidence of this, but there were clear signs that Andy had struck the ledge at the top of pitch 1 on his way to the ground, so his impact may have dislodged the rocks there.

There is circumstantial evidence that Andy's state of mind may have set him up for an accident. First, he seemed to be in an unenthusiastic mood that day, perhaps feeling ill. Second, although he was an experienced free climber, he had little aid experience and had complained of being inefficient with his big wall ascenders. Third, he had been struggling with his rappel ropes for an hour or two, clearly annoyed by the situation. Each problem, by itself, may have been frustrating but was not necessarily dangerous per se; however, one irritation on top of another may have ultimately led to hasty decisions and shortcuts with safety. Of course we cannot know Andy's state of mind; the possibility of contributing mental factors is offered here for other climbers to watch for in themselves.

In summary, the most likely scenario places Andy at or near the bottom of the first rappel from Dinner Ledge, trying to free his jammed rappel ropes by pulling hard on one rope. When the rope suddenly came loose, he lost his balance and fell, pulling the other rope through the anchor above and taking both ropes with him.

While we do not know exactly what Andy was doing at the time, or what caused his fall, we can be fairly certain that for whatever reason, either he had no anchor to the cliff at that moment or he had fashioned an inadequate one.

Several observations have been left out of this analysis for lack of space. Note that none of the key skills involved in this accident are unique to big-wall climbs. Ascending and freeing jammed rappel ropes and maintaining a secure tie-in are concepts important to free climbing as well. (Source: John Dill, NPS Ranger, Yosemite National Park)

VARIOUS FALLS ON ROCK, VARIOUS CAUSES
California, Joshua Tree National Park

There were five incident reports from this park that qualified for the data. They all were falls, three of them resulting in injuries because either protection pulled or there was inadequate protection. One fall resulted on a lowering—when the belay rope whistled through the stitch-plate belay device. Another occurred when a husband was rappelling from the same (doubled) rope his wife was climbing on. She had no belay when she fell.

There were, as usual, hikers getting into technical terrain and falling. Two of these fell 50 feet. (Source: Incident Reports submitted by Joshua Tree National Park)

WEATHER—HIGH WINDS, FALL ON TO ROCKS
Colorado, Rocky Mountain National Park, Longs Peak

On February 7, Craig Dreher (30) and Gene Williamson (30) decided to abort their winter attempt of the Keyhole Route due to high winds. As they were retreating from the Boulder Field, a gust of westerly wind estimated at 150 mph knocked over Williamson and picked up Dreher (who weighs 170 pounds) free of the ground. Dreher was tossed into a pile of rocks, impacting on his right ankle, resulting in a fracture of the fibula.

Analysis

Although this accident occurred on non-technical terrain, Dreher and Williamson requested that this be brought to the readers' attention as an example of the high wind hazard prevalent on winter climbs of Longs Peak. Winds have been twice measured on the Longs Peak summit at 220 mph. It should also be mentioned that Dreher was wearing a 70-pound pack when picked up by the wind! Dreher and Williamson showed good judgment in aborting their summit attempt in these conditions. (Source: Jim Detterline and Mark Magnuson, NPS Rangers, RMNP)

FALL ON ROCK, NO HARD HAT, EXCEEDING ABILITIES
Colorado, Boulder Canyon, Happy Hour Crag

On February 26, while lead climbing in Boulder Canyon with two relatively inexperienced members in my group, I lent my helmet to Rob, the least experienced person in our group (who had never climbed outdoors before). Darin, our most experienced climber, was climbing a 5.8-5.9 buttress immediately west of our established position, while being belayed by Dave (who had a great deal of experience in the gym, but likewise had never been outdoors before). Lance belayed me on a route that looked like it might have been 5.6-soft 5.7. Rob was going to top-rope the route. For the first 80 feet of the route, I placed pro approximately every 10 to 15 feet. The route arced from left to right. My final pro placement was a threaded sling through a pothole, from which I had a 30-foot traverse to the natural anchor. Within 10 feet of the anchor, I slipped and fell about 25-30 feet, hitting the top of my head on the rock face. Lance made a sure-handed catch, but I had lacerated my scalp. The copious blood flow impressed upon me the necessity of being examined by a medical professional. Lance accompanied me during the short down-climb/rappel and drove me to the Boulder Community Hospital, where I received seven stitches to close the laceration on my scalp.

Analysis

I clearly should have worn my helmet, especially while on lead. My reason for leaving my helmet with Rob (so he might climb with a greater feeling of security) demonstrates that I began the climb without a clear idea of whether the second was going to follow me up to the natural anchor, from which we would continue up, or if he was merely going to top-rope. I had obviously underestimated the difficulty of the route and/or overestimated my own ability. Further, the arcing route I took made the problem of rope drag a factor, which may or may not have contributed to me falling in the first place.

You can be certain that I will never again climb, let alone lead, without wearing my helmet. (Source: Jon Canon - 28)

FALL ON ROCK, INADEQUATE TIE-IN FOR LOWERING, NO HARD HAT
Colorado, Clear Creek Canyon, Cat Slab

On April 24, Heather Lower (25) died in Clear Creek Canyon. She was climbing west of Tunnel 5. (A few areas there include: Cat Slab, Dog House, Primo Wall, and Crystal Tower.) She was with eight others. She fell 100-125 feet. She was not wearing a helmet. She was pronounced dead at the scene.

Analysis

She was at Cat Slab, a new 5.4-5.10 bolted slab where folks often anchor themselves and thread the anchors to lower/rap. She was about to be lowered and apparently unclipped the wrong figure-8 on a bight loop from her harness and then failed to check that she was indeed on belay to be lowered off using a sling-shot belay. Tying in directly to the harness avoids this kind of problem. (Source: Leo Paik and Bill May)

(Editor's Note: There was another fatality at this area earlier in the year. The little information we have suggests that, as in the above case, the climber was being lowered and the system didn't work, because he dropped 60 feet. Unfortunately, lowering incidents like this are on the increase. See the next one!)

FALL ON ROCK, INADEQUATE ANCHOR ON TOP ROPE SET UP
Colorado, Boulder Canyon, Happy Hour Crag

On April 20, a climber fell to his death while being lowered, due to the webbing on one of the anchor's parting and not being properly clipped in to the equalizing anchor. In the case of the webbing, it was only masking tape that connected (and hid!) the ends of one of two webbing anchor slings. This accident was particularly noteworthy because the climber had purchased the webbing the day before and did not realize that masking tape joined two pieces of webbing. The webbing came off the spool that did not have one continuous length. (Source: Bill May)

(Editor's Note: This kind of mistake has only been reported once before to ANAM— many years ago. It is —or should be—fairly common knowledge that webbing, unlike rope, comes packaged in this manner.)

SNOW BLINDNESS—INADEQUATE EQUIPMENT
Colorado, Rocky Mountain National Park, Longs Peak

On June 11, Michael William Pope (45) lost his sight while descending from a successful off-season ascent of the Keyhole Route on Longs Peak. It was a particularly bright and sunny day on the snow-covered route, but Pope had forgotten to pack his sunglasses. His eyes began to burn with intense pain, and he could not see farther than 10 feet. What he could see was blurred with a milky haze to it. Pope called for assistance through his family band radio. Park rangers responded and assisted him to the trailhead.

Analysis

Losing one's sight on a mountain can result in additional accidents! Remember your sunglasses or turn around before the damage to your eyes becomes severe. In an emergency, one can manufacture an improvised pair of sunglasses from cardboard and/or tape with just small slits for viewing. (Source: Jim Detterline and Mark Magnuson, NPS Rangers, RMNP)

FALL OR SLIP ON ROCK—TWO INCIDENTS
Colorado, Black Canyon of the Gunnison

On June 17, Zach Alberts (20) fell while leading a climb of the 5.10+ Cruise route. Alberts was climbing about 10 feet above his last piece of protection when he lost his footing, slipped and fell, sustaining possible fractures to both ankles. Alberts' climbing partner contacted North Rim Ranger Ed Delmolino at 9:30 p.m. Delmolino treated Alberts' injuries and monitored his condition through the night until rescue operations could begin the following morning. Park and local rescue teams raised Alberts up the North Chasm wall over 1,500 feet to the rim of the canyon. The mission took about five hours and over 25 rescuers to complete. Marion Parker was IC.

On July 9, Martha Moses (41) fell while lead-climbing Cruise Gully after she and her partner abandoned a climb on the Leisure route. Moses was climbing 50 feet above her first protection in intermittent rain when she apparently lost her footing, fell and tumbled about 80 feet, sustaining severe head injuries. Her partner contacted ranger Ed Delmolino, who responded along with a paramedic from a local EMS squad.

The nighttime litter evacuation involved lowering her down the remainder of the gully in rain, lightning, and continuous rock falls. Moses was then raised over 1,500 feet up the North Chasm wall to the rim and flown by helicopter to St. Mary's Hospital in Grand Junction, where she underwent surgery for a skull fracture.

The entire operation took 12 hours and involved 50 rescuers and support personnel, including a number of local, county, and volunteer rescue squads. These two operations constitute the most significant technical raises to date in the park. (Source: Linda Alick, Black Canyon of the Gunnison)

(Editor's Note: These are the first reports from Black Canyon in a long time. It is interesting to note their final comment, which might explain this.)

FALLING ICE
Colorado, Rocky Mountain National Park, Longs Peak
On June 25, Jesse Woods (20) and Scott Kastengren were preparing to climb the third pitch of the Casual Route (IV 5.10) on the Diamond of Longs Peak when Woods was struck in the face by falling ice. He sustained lacerations to the forehead (requiring 22 sutures), a concussion, fractured nose, and hematomas surrounding both eyes. Kastengren lowered Woods back down to Broadway Ledge where they were assisted by two other climbers known as Al and Craig. At Mills Glacier they were joined by park rescue for a helicopter evacuation.

Analysis
Late spring and early summer bring the highest incidence of falling ice with the advent of longer days and warmer temperatures. However, it is possible to encounter falling ice and falling rock (due to freeze/thaw cycles) at any other time of year on Longs Peak depending on conditions. While it is sometimes possible to gauge the hazard by inspecting the upper face with binoculars, there is no certain way to predict the risk of falling ice here.

Woods was wearing his helmet and was clipped into the belay anchors at the time of the accident, preventing more serious consequences. Woods and Kastengren, with the assistance of fellow climbers who kindly assisted in the spirit of true mountaineers, did an excellent job in evacuating from the Diamond and Lower East Face. (Source: Jim Detterline and Mark Magnuson, NPS Rangers, RMNP)

FALL ON ROCK, INADEQUATE PROTECTION—PULLED OUT, LATE START— IMPENDING DARKNESS, OFF ROUTE, INEXPERIENCE
Colorado, Rocky Mountain National Park, The Book

On July 1, Mike Head (26) and Levois "Adolph" Garcia were attempting to climb Osiris (II 5.7) on The Book. Head, the leader, got off route on the final pitch and fell from a section of 5.10 rock as he was attempting to place protection. He pulled the next piece of protection out as he fell, sustaining a 50-foot fall and fracturing three bones in his right foot. He anchored himself to a small tree and called for Garcia to ascend to him, but Garcia was unable to climb up to Head. Head used his cell phone to contact park rescue, who responded with a night cliff evacuation. Head's fractures were extensive, requiring surgery and a cast for two to three months.

Analysis

There were a number of smaller factors coupled with the relative inexperience of this party that led up to this accident. The pair had a guidebook with them, but did not refer to it during the climb. They started rather late—at 1530—for a four-pitch climb, plus a two-mile walk back to the car. Finally, although Head was dealing very well with his first 5.10 lead, he unfortunately fell before he could clip the piece, and then the next lower piece was inadequately placed to hold a fall. Head said that he did feel rushed on this pitch with impending darkness, so this was also a factor. (Source: Jim Detterline and Mark Magnuson, NPS Rangers, RMNP)

FALL ON ROCK, CLIMBING UNROPED—TRYING TO SAVE TIME
Colorado, Rocky Mountain National Park, Longs Peak

On July 6, Cameron Tague (32) and Emma Williams (34) were attempting the Yellow Wall Route (V 5.11) on the Diamond of Longs Peak. Tague was climbing unroped on a steep band of rotten 4th class rock at the base of the Yellow Wall Route looking for a belay on better rock. Tague slipped on loose rock and fell 800 feet to his death over the Lower East Face and onto Mills Glacier.

Analysis

Tague was an outstanding climber with approximately 30 ascents of routes on the Diamond face, including a new route. His strategy in climbing unroped was to save time and increase his party's margin of safety later in the day by finishing the route before the afternoon lightning storms would arrive. However, in retrospect, it may have been better to simul-climb with protection placed at intervals. The North Chimney (access route to the Diamond) and Broadway Ledge are notorious for rotten rock, conditions that have claimed other capable climbers in these same areas. (Source: Jim Detterline and Mark Magnuson, NPS Rangers, RMNP)

LIGHTNING, POOR POSITION—LATE AFTERNOON
Colorado, Rocky Mountain National Park, Longs Peak

On July 12, Andy Haberkorn (28) was seconding his partner, Stanley Smigel, on a crux 5.10 pitch of the Casual Route on the Diamond of Longs Peak. As

Haberkorn was about 40 feet above the Yellow Wall bivouac ledge, a bright flash of lightning was observed by Smigel in the vicinity of Haberkorn. Haberkorn had received a fatal lightning strike which entered his chest. Smigel was able to respond to his partner briefly, but Haberkorn had succumbed to his internal injuries.

Analysis

Lighting is common element of the Colorado Rockies high country. Haberkorn's fatal strike occurred about 1500, a most dangerous time of day to be high on the face in midsummer. It was during a rather unsettled period, where lightning storms were more common than normal.

Planning your route so that you can be up and down prior to 1300 is prudent, even though the attempt might not necessarily be successful. There is a past history of a climber struck by lightning at this same spot. Usually lightning strikes the summit and outstanding points on ridges. Also, lightning usually strikes the leader or higher individual. Mr. Smigel must be commended for his efforts in tending to his partner, and in getting down the Diamond under the most difficult conditions. (Source: Jim Detterline and Mark Magnuson, NPS Rangers, RMNP)

FALL ON ROCK, PROTECTION PULLED OUT
Colorado, Eldorado State Park, Bastille Rock

On July 27, Aaron Nydam (24) sustained a dislocated hip and cuts on his leg after falling about 25 feet while climbing with his brothers Scott and Trevor. His climbing protection came out. Soldiers from Fort Carson were training in the area and helped after the fall. He was take to Boulder Community Hospital for observation. (Source: From a newspaper clipping in the *Rocky Mountain News*, sent in by Leo Paik)

FALL ON ROCK, INADEQUATE PROTECTION
Colorado, Rocky Mountain National Park, Longs Peak

On August 5, James A. Guest (32) took a 30-foot lead fall on Pervertical Sanctuary (V 5.10) on the Diamond of Longs Peak. Guest impacted hard against both feet, resulting in fractures to both legs. His partner, Brent Moore, assisted by additional Diamond climbers Charles Lewinsohn and Eric Wass, lowered Guest down the 800-foot Lower East Face to Mills Glacier, where they were met by the park rescue team for a helicopter evacuations.

Analysis

Guest's protection did arrest his fall, but had that protection been closer to the fall initiation point, he might not have attained the destructive force necessary to fracture both legs. Guest and Moore did a fantastic job with self-rescue, which emphasizes the importance of studying these skills. Most endearing is the example of Lewinsohn and Wass, who showed that the code of the mountains (drop your goal to help a fellow climber in need) is alive and well. (Source: Jim Detterline and Mark Magnuson, NPS Rangers, RMNP)

FALL ON SNOW, LOSS OF CONTROL–VOLUNTARY GLISSADE, INEXPERIENCE
Colorado, Rocky Mountain National Park, Mount Ypsilon

On August 26, Larisa J. Watson (23) and three partners partially ascended the Blitzen Ridge route on Mount Ypsilon when they noticed incoming foul weather and decided to retreat. While glissading the Spectacle Lake Snowfield, Watson lost control and slid 150 feet, impacting on rocks at the bottom of the snowfield. She sustained head and facial injuries, resulting in a two-day rescue effort.

Analysis

Watson was not as experienced as the other team members, and was not familiar with glissading. The team leader glissaded first, but was without an ax. He attempted to stop Watson but aborted when he also began to lose control. The other team members wisely descended by cutting steps. (Source: Jim Detterline and Mark Magnuson, NPS Rangers, RMNP)

OVERDUE, WEATHER, EXHAUSTION, EXCEEDING ABILITIES
Colorado, Rocky Mountain National Park, Longs Peak

On October 21, RMNP dispatch received a missing/overdue climbing party report concerning John McBroom (47) and Terrance Ford (42) on Kiener's Route (III AI), Longs Peak. They were to have returned home on October 20. Searchers were dispatched to the mountain, and they located McBroom and Ford exhausted but otherwise uninjured.

Analysis

McBroom and Ford were the third party within two weeks to have endured an unplanned bivouac on Kiener's Route, resulting in a 40-hour climb and descent of the peak. Similar incidents also have commonly occurred here at this time of the season in other years, resulting in cold injuries and even death. We present this case in the interest of preventing future episodes. Each overdue party underestimated the increased difficulty of the route caused by early winter conditions. Under summer conditions Kiener's Route is a mountaineering classic of easy 5th class climbing and 40- to 50-degree snow and ice. Early winter snows had covered the route with up to 20 inches of poorly-bonded snow resulting in climbing difficulties well beyond those of summer. Also, many groups experience route-finding difficulties due to winter conditions and inexperience. An off-season Kiener's climb requires a conservative attitude. (Source: Jim Detterline and Mark Magnuson, NPS Rangers, RMNP)

(Editor's Note: Tim Ashwood asked us to print a clarification of a few details regarding his accident on Longs Peak reported last year on page 56 of ANAM.

"Here is what happened. The last night we spent on the Diamond we were about 200 feet from the top of the Diamond. The game plan was to finish the Diamond then go the last 200 feet to the top of the mountain, get back down, clean the gear off the Diamond, and get to the boulder field before the afternoon storms. That night I got sick from some bad food and spent the night throwing up several times. By the next day I had no more food or water in my system and my throat felt like needles sticking it. The quickest way off the Diamond and back down at that time was to go the last 200 feet up, since we already had ropes strung to the top of The Diamond. We had been cleaning up the gear as we went up so we didn't have any gear set up below us. Since I was so sick, we didn't go to the top of the mountain, just the Diamond, then headed straight down to our base camp at Chasm View. We spent the night at Chasm View since it started to storm, then headed down to the boulder field the next morning to meet the Ranger and the horse. I tried to drink a little water, but would just throw it back up; my system would not hold even water down for very long.

I spent about six weeks training in Estes Park, Colorado, before the Diamond push. My cerebral palsy improved so much, I was doing things at the end of the summer I couldn't do at the beginning of the summer. This was my third attempt. The first two were turned back because of weather and time. The third time we allotted 10 days to do the climb in hopes of finding the correct weather window, so there was 'no attitude to summit at all costs' as stated.

Also, there was no ambulance involved. A friend took me to the hospital, where I was treated for food poisoning, which is what caused the low energy levels, nausea, and dehydration, not my cerebral palsy or the inability of my partners and me. When I got back down to the trailhead, my voice was almost gone so I wasn't able to give much detail on what happened to Jim Detterline.")

VARIOUS FALLS ON ROCK
Idaho, City of Rocks National Reserve
This year we only had four reported climbing accidents. Two of these came to our attention only because the parties involved stopped by the Visitor Center to ask for directions to the hospital.

Daniel Hansen (22) fell while attempting Dynamo Hum, a popular 5.10c on Transformer Wall. He missed the correct start and fell from about eight feet up, landing on an erosion control retaining wall. He fractured and dislocated his ankle. This terrace was intentionally positioned such that it would provide a good landing zone should someone come off the start of the route—but not so good a landing zone for Daniel's "variation."

The second accident—which was a self-rescue—happened to Ian McNeill, who sustained a hip injury falling from New Troy, a notorious 5.10cR on Super Hits Wall. We do not know the details, but a fall from the crux would result in a 20-foot-plus ground fall. McNeill may have overestimated his abilities.

The other two involved rescue efforts by City of Rocks personnel. The first one was to Jamie Aghain (35), who was scrambling down the gully from the Crack House at Castle Rocks when he popped a hold and fell head first into a crevice between two boulders. He sustained a subdural hematoma. He was lucky to be in the company of an ER physician and that there happened to be other experienced rescue personnel nearby—because on any given day, there would have been no one within miles, as Castle Rocks is not open to the public yet. Also, Jamie may have walked away from this if he had been wearing a helmet.

The last incident was also in an area that is closed to the public. Robert Laymon (38) fell while climbing unroped on the controversial North Twin Sister, the closer of which has been the object of years of legal battles between the Access Fund and NPS. It is unknown how far Mr. Laymon fell, but his injuries would suggest that he took quite a tumble. He may have fallen due at least in part from distraction, as there was a major wildfire just south of the Sister, which, in fact, was forcing a general evacuation from the Reserve! (Source: From a letter and reports sent by Brad Shilling, Climbing Ranger)

RAPPEL FAILURE
Illinois, Mississippi Palisades Park, Sentinel Rock
In November, Steven Wallace (27) died in hospital following his 40 foot fall from Sentinel Rock, from which he was rappelling. No other details were available, but as this is an area now used by climbers, it is important to call attention to it, especially as a fatality occurred. (Source: From a report sent in by Budge Gierke)

FALL OR SLIP ON ROCK, PROTECTION FAILURE
North Carolina, Looking Glass Rock, Second Coming
On May 5, Ben Williams (21) and his partner were attempting Second Coming (5.7), a popular route on the south side of Looking Glass Rock. He was wearing a helmet. Williams, a climber with 1-3 years experience, placed several pieces of gear as he climbed the crack below the bulge (crux). Standing beneath the bulge, he placed a #2 Camalot as high as he could reach into the vertical crack that splits the bulge. From this position, he attempted to climb upwards, moving his foot out to the right of the crack. Finding no place for his toe, he slipped and fell back and to the left below the bulge. This caused the #2 Camalot placement to fail. His fall was stopped by a well-placed #.5 Camalot. Some time during the fall, Williams stuck his ankle, breaking it. An evacuation by Transylvania County EMS and volunteers was necessary. Williams was in a great deal of pain, even though he was sedated with morphine. The carry-out was difficult from both his standpoint and that of the rescuers.
Analysis
Williams was lead climbing on the route that some call the most dangerous climb (from a serious injury standpoint) at Looking Glass Rock. One explanation may be that new climbers, often not skilled at placing "trad" gear, are sandbagged by the 5.7 rating that appears in the guidebook. That, plus the fact the "Second Coming" starts with a benign-appearing crack that suckers the climber into believing that it will continue being as easy as it seems at the beginning. Poorly-placed gear near the "bulge," nervousness when actually attempting to climb it, pro that fails to hold when loaded with a climber's weight—all of these factors figure into the frequency/severity of injuries that take place on the route. In Ben's case, he had fallen at the same spot two weeks

prior to his injury in May. The difference was that on his first fall at the crux, the piece, a #2 Camalot, held. On May 5th, it pulled. Why didn't it fail the first time he fell? Most likely because Ben took more time in placing it properly when he first encountered that spot. During the May 5 climb, he may have placed the Camalot too quickly and carelessly, assuming first that he knew what he was doing because he had fallen on the same piece at the same place before and all went well, and second that on this "return" visit to the route, he was READY TO CLIMB and did not expect to fall again.

Familiarity and practice placing gear, better position, and anticipation of "what if this piece pulls" may have prepared the climber for the unexpected. (Source: Ben Williams and Steve Longnecker)

FALL ON ROCK, PROTECTION FAILURE
North Carolina, Looking Glass Rock, The Womb.

Ian Randall (26) and I, Josh Whitmore (23), both experienced climbers were climbing The Womb (5.11) on the north side of Looking Glass Rock on June 9. The accident occurred on the first pitch. I was approximately 40 feet off the ground with a cam placed at foot level when I fell. The piece pulled and I fell to the ground landing in a seated position on a boulder at the base of the climb, followed by a roll onto the ground. I never hit my head. (I was wearing a helmet.) I experienced extreme pain in my coccyx and in the center of my back. Both Ian and I are Wilderness First Responders. He log-rolled me into a position on my back, completed primary and secondary surveys, stabilized me the best he could and went for help. There was no one else in the area.

One-and-a-half hours later, Ian returned with the local rescue squad who packaged me onto a backboard and litter, transporting me to a trailhead approximately two miles away. Members of the Schenck Job Corps and two North Carolina Outward Bound crews also assisted in the litter carry.

Analysis

Forty feet seems like a long way up to have placed just one piece of protection, but due to the nature of the climb it was reasonable. The first 30 feet of the climb is a gently sloping slab (5.3-5.4) that offers no protection. The route then traverses up and right above steeper rock. This section is considerably harder but offers good protection. I climbed the easy section, placed a piece to protect myself for 3-4 feet of climbing to a rest stance. I placed a second piece (a mid-sized cam) as high as I could reach. I knew that I needed the first piece higher at the crux, so I backed cleaned it. This left me with only one placement, the mid-sized cam that was well placed in a horizontal crack. I went back and forth several times in the next section trying to work out the sequence. When I fell, I was in the process of down-climbing. I believe that the piece pulled because it had "walked" into a bad position from its original good placement due to the back and forth movement of the rope running through the protection carabiner.

In hindsight, there are a number of things that could have been done differently that may have prevented the piece from pulling. A long runner on the cam would have created less drag, allowing the rope to run "smoother." The cam could have been placed deeper into the crack to prevent "walking." I could have placed more than one piece in opposition, equalized two pieces, or not back cleaned the first piece. One large lesson I learned is that the first piece needs to be a bomber placement, multidirectional, and minimal potential for "walking." (Source: Josh Whitmore)

FALL OR SLIP ON ICE, ICE SCREW PULLED OUT, HASTE
North Carolina, Celo Knob, The Crescent

(The month of December was one of the coldest on record in North Carolina. The below-freezing temperatures created a variety of great ice climbing opportunities throughout the western part of the state.)

Around 3:00 p.m., my partner TS and I were finishing our second ice route of the day in the Black Mountain Range. Both routes were characteristic of the long gully climbs—easy to moderate ice with a few technical stretches no harder than WI3. I was beginning the last of the roped pitches, a short 30-foot section of relatively easy WI3. I had placed a good screw just off the belay, and then placed a second one five more feet above. I encountered a short section of névé near the end of the pitch which felt secure, although warranted some delicate climbing. To protect the top-out, I placed a third screw in the best ice I could find, knowing that it was not very solid but hoping it would be better than nothing. The angle lessened considerably at the top of the pitch, transforming into a flat ramp that continued towards the top of the mountain. After making a few more moves past the vertical section, I stepped up high to plant my left foot flat into the ice and finish the pitch using my tools as canes on such low-angle terrain. I planted the bottom of both tools into the ice and committed my weight onto my left foot when it skated off the ice, pitching me off backwards in a head-first fall. I remember the last screw failing as I fell and could see the ledge below me coming closer and closer. I hit the ledge with my head and shoulder blade, bounced, and continued to slide 20 more feet down the gully until I came to a halt. By the time I stopped, I had fallen 40 feet, dislocated my left shoulder, and stabbed my right knee with my crampon during the fall. TS came down to help me out and managed to reduce my shoulder. He pulled all our gear and helped me bushwhack several hundred feet down the ridge to our packs and walk the remaining miles back to the truck.

Analysis

More so than climbing on rock, ice climbing takes keen judgment and the experience to know what is happening with the ice and what techniques are and are not safe. A contributing factor to my fall was rushing the pitch and wanting to get off the mountain after a long day. If I had continued to climb the pitch in the standard manner of planting the picks of both tools *firmly* before making a move instead of hastily resorting to a more efficient technique, I might not have fallen. Also, if I had not been wearing a helmet, I might not have lived to tell this tale. (Source: Brandon Calloway - 28)

RAPPEL FAILURE–ANCHOR CAME AWAY, INADEQUATE PROTECTION
New Jersey, Mount Tammany, Delaware Water Gap National Recreation Area

Steve Raible (22) fell about 120 feet to his death while rappelling from a route on Mount Raible and climbing partner Todd Garcia had completed a technical climb of "Double Overhang" (5.8) and were in the process of rappelling from the top when the accident occurred at 7:15 p.m. According to Garcia, Raible was rappelling on a double-rope, utilizing a sling on a resident rappel station. Garcia told NPS investigators that Raible had descended about 15 feet when the anchor failed, causing him to fall to the ground. Garcia descended and checked Raible, but could not detect either a pulse or breath.

Garcia then descended to a scree slope and then to a nearby highway where he flagged down a passing motorist. The motorist used his cell phone to make a 911 call. A state trooper and local fire and EMS reached the scene at 8:20 p.m. They found that Raible had suffered extensive and severe traumatic injuries and had no pulse or respirations. A carry-out of the victim's body was completed after midnight by the Park's high-angle rescue team and a township search and rescue squad.

Analysis

The fixed rappel station, located in the middle of the cliff consisted of resident webbing threaded through a crack and around a block. Garcia and Raible examined and tested the webbing, judging it to be safe. No back-up was used.

It is noteworthy to say that the webbing held Raible's full body weight as he rapelled 15 feet down the face; therefore, no amount of testing could have produced the failure of the webbing.

ALWAYS back up resident rappel stations! In this case, it was not possible to thread new webbing through the existing crack, but a backup using our gear should have been used. (Source: From a report by Todd Garcia)

FALL ON ROCK–TESTING PROTECTION WHICH PULLED OUT AND FALLING ROCK
New Mexico, Sandia Mountains, The Shield

After a long approach on August 26, four well-prepared and experienced climbers began to climb the six-pitch Standard "S" Route (IV 5.6) on The Shield, the largest wall in the Sandia Mountains outside of Albuquerque. About 650 feet from the top, the 40-year-old male lead climber had just placed several pieces. Holding onto a small ledge with his left hand and standing on both feet, he was testing a nut by pulling on it to see how it would hold. Without warning the piece popped out and he was thrown off balance, lost his grip on the rock, and fell backward becoming airborne. The cam below him was loaded with the leader fall and failed under the force. He fell directly onto his right posterior lower rib cage on a ledge approximately 15 feet below him and then continued to fall another 10 feet until the belayer was able to arrest the fall. The leader did not lose consciousness and was able to be lowered to the belay ledge. However, he was unable to move because of chest wall and abdominal pain and was short of breath.

One of the climbing party members had his cell phone and radio to call for help, and he also happens to be an active member of Albuquerque Mountain Rescue. A rescue was initiated which included mutual-aid from the Army National Guard, Air Force Pararescue, and other SAR teams.

A 600-foot rope was used to begin access from the top. A Sked litter was air lifted to the strike team on the face by a Blackhawk helicopter. One of the climbers had led another pitch and the 9mm dynamic rope was tied to the 600-foot static rope in order to access the patient another 50 feet further down.

The patient was complaining of shortness of breath, chest wall pain, abdominal pain, and numbness in his feet. The initial assessment of the patient revealed possible rib fractures, fractured lumbar spine, and retroperitoneal hemorrhage, all of which were later diagnosed in the hospital. A litter hoist could not be effected from the ledge because of how close it would place the helicopter to the rock in moderate and shifty winds. An attempt was made of putting the patient into the Sked and lowering him to a more accessible ledge was unsuccessful because of low light limitations. The patient was brought back up to the initial point of contact and the patient was transferred into a Stokes litter and vacuum splint for the 650-foot-high angle technical raise to the top of the Shield. The paramedics on the strike team started an IV line and morphine was given for pain before the transfer and technical raise.

The top is a narrow 15-foot-wide ridge with 1000-foot exposure on both sides. The haul system included a 90-degree change of direction that went up the ridge to the haul team. During the course of the haul, some carabiners on the change of direction pulley were loaded awkwardly which forced that gates to pop open and place the litter team in some danger. However, a second belay line was already attached if the haul system failed.

Two litter bearers were used in a difficult dihedral loaded with overhangs and lose rock. At the last part of the raise, a rock was accidentally knocked lose by the litter team. The rock crashed down through the dihedral system. "Rock, rock... everyone get close to the wall," was called out on the radio, but one of the other climbers on the climbing team was struck on the thigh, suffering a bruise that would prohibit her from climbing out.

A hoist from the Blackhawk was done with night vision capabilities off the top of the Shield and the patient was taken to University Hospital. Air Force Pararescue Team members lowered the 40-year-old female over 800 feet to the base of the Shield and she was airlifted out the next morning. (Source: J. Marc Beverly, WEMT-P, Albuquerque Mountain Rescue)

AVALANCHE, POOR POSITION
New York, Adirondack High Peaks, Wright Peak

On February 20, one skier was killed and five others injured when they were caught in an avalanche in the Adirondack High Peaks while skiing in an off-trail area. The avalanche occurred about 1:00 p.m. on the northeast side of Wright Peak. Department of Environmental Conservation Forest Rangers (MRA) reported that five of the skiers were found by 2:00 p.m. Searchers spent the next five hours looking for Toma Jacob Vracarich (27). Using a probe line, they finally found his body around 6:00 p.m. Of the five injured skiers, three were hospitalized.

Very high snow levels had created unusual avalanche conditions in the northeast. DEC Ranger Wesley Hurd: "In New York State we never have avalanches. I've been doing this for 26 years and this is the first one I've ever had anything to do with that had any people involved." In Vermont, state officials told Stowe Mountain Resort and Smuggler's Notch Ski Area to warn backcountry skiers and snowboarders of significant risk of avalanche in Smuggler's Notch. (Source: Neil Van Dyke, Stowe Hazardous Terrain Evacuation)

(Editor's Note: This incident is included because backcountry skiing and snowboarding are becoming more popular in the Northeast. It is important to understand the conditions that can result in avalanches.)

VARIOUS LEADER FALLS ON ROCK, PROTECTION PULLED OUT (4), INADEQUATE PROTECTION (2), OLD WEBBING BROKE WHEN WEIGHTED (1)
New York, Mohonk Preserve, Shawangunks

There were 17 climbing incidents reported from the Preserve this year. Fourteen happened to lead climbers and three while bouldering. The latter would be considered "normal" falls, though they resulted in sprains because of the way the climbers landed. Several of the lead climbing incidents were exacerbated because protection was inadequate or came out. One leader was 20 feet from the top when she was bitten by a snake (species unknown), but suffered no serious consequence. One cliff rescue was performed from the Grand Traverse ledge in the Trapps. A climber (31) attempting to begin the third pitch of the popular Andrew (5.4) got off route and wandered into Three Vultures (5.9). As the leader attempted to aid through a move by grabbing an old piece of sling attached to a piton (hints at the age), the sling broke, resulting in a fall of about 30 feet with impact to the cliff. He was lowered to the GT ledge by his belayer, lowered off the cliff in a litter by rangers, carried down the talus and taken to an ambulance via ranger truck. He sustained a fractured pelvis (in three places) and fibula, and required stitches on a laceration to his left knee.

One case to note occurred to a man (66) who is a veteran of the cliffs. He was starting up on a fairly easy climb—Three Pines—but had placed only one piece of protection. He was 20 feet up when he fell. His protection came out, so he hit the ground and tumbled additional distance, crushing his pelvis. However, he feels strongly that his helmet saved him from possible death or at the very least mental debilitation. It is to be noted that of all the incidents reported, in only two cases were helmets being worn. A final observation: The average age of those involved in leader falls was 37! The graying of the Gunks. (Source: From the Annual Report submitted by the Mohonk Preserve and Jed Williamson)

FALL ON ROCK, INADEQUATE PROTECTION—FAILURE TO ASSESS ROCK FORMATION, INADEQUATE BELAY, EXCEEDING ABILITIES, FAILURE TO FOLLOW ROUTE
Oregon, Mount Washington

At sunrise on June 29, Eric Seyler (28) and Kurt Smith (26) left their bivouac high on the North Ridge of Mount Washington to climb Central Pillar, described in their guide book, "*Oregon High*", by Jeff Thomas, as "steep, exposed and a joy to climb." Unable to identify the described route positively, they chose a line that looked promising. At the top of the first 90-foot pitch of blocky, straightforward rock, Eric arrived at rappel slings looped between a fixed piton and a large block. He replaced the slings with a single spectra sling stretched horizontally around the block between the fixed piton and a new passive nut placement. He belayed Kurt to a ledge below and clove hitched Kurt to the single nut at one side of the sling. Kurt set two small passive nuts and attached each of them to his harness. As Eric climbed on, he clipped the rope to one side of the spectra sling as a first point of protection above his belayer. He set three more passive nuts for protection as he continued. Shortly after, Eric and Kurt fell more than 100 feet to hard sloping snow after the spectra sling broke and each piece of gear they had set in the brittle volcanic rock tore out. Both young men lay in agony with broken legs and other very serious injuries for three cold days in the wind and burning sun and two frigid nights high in the Mount Washington Wilderness. By luck alone, their whistle was heard by two Saturday hikers with radio and telephone contact to the Deschutes County SAR and soon after, by four members of the Eugene Mountain Rescue team on a personal outing, perhaps the only climbers on the mountain that weekend. Late in the day, they were airlifted out by USAF Reserve helicopter that was guided in by a cell phone patch.

Analysis

The conversion of sport climbing skills to mountaineering is perceived by alpinists to be full of dangers. Wilderness mountaineering at 7,500 feet requires a significant investment of effort and experience to balance the risk. At guide book-rated 5.8, Eric believed this route was well within his capabilities. He had been sport climbing for several years, but leading traditional for about two years at 5.9+ at Broughton Bluff, a local crag. This was essentially his first wilderness rock route. Guidebook generalities must be interpreted with cautious experience on less-than-perfect alpine rock.

Eric now realizes he made a grave error in not creating an equalized, narrow angled, no extension, redundant, bombproof belay anchor. As he fell, all of the force came on one nut at a time in sequence as his protection pulled from the rock. He then broke the single spectra sling stretched 120 degrees horizontally and clipped in "an American triangle" only on one side as it raked across the rough volcanic rock. As he pulled his belayer off the ledge, the single medium-sized anchor nut and two small brass nuts exploded from the rock.

Kurt considers his mistake to be his silence. He felt that they should try an easier adjoining route but was silent; he thought the rock looked bad, but did not say so and he did not insist on checking his belay anchor and the first placement protecting him above his belay ledge.

The novice alpinists made two additional mistakes. They had told friends where they were going, but they did not say, "So, if we don't make it back by then, call the Search and Rescue right away." And they left their cell phone in the car. (They did not know that the smallest cell phones work very well in the high Oregon Cascades.)

"At some point, I made a statement John Wayne would have been proud of: 'The only way we'll get through this is Courage,'" wrote Eric Seyler in an article he called "Playing Icarus on Mount Washington."

The most important thing that can be learned from this accident is how companions can support each other and prevail over unimaginable hardship. Eric and Kurt are continuing to recover from their serious injuries and infections. Medical personnel are amazed that Eric and Kurt did not die on the mountain from shock from their terrible injuries. (Source: Robert L. Speik)

FALL ON SNOW—UNROPED AT SUMMIT, WIND
Oregon, Mount Hood
On June 4, Diana Kornet (29) slipped as she was looking over the northeast side of Mount Hood. She fell about 2,500 feet to her death. She and six friends had reached the summit about 7 a.m. She unroped—as many climbers do—and left her ice ax when she went to take a look. It was windy in this exposed location. (Source: From articles in *The Oregonian* and Jeff Sheetz)

FALL ON ROCK
Oregon, Mount Hood, Sandy Glacier Headwall
On June 20, James Frankenfield (39) and Iain Morris (23) were on the Sandy Glacier Headwall route on Mount Hood. At 0730, while traversing above the glacier to the headwall, they were involved in a major rockfall event which initiated thousands of feet above on the upper buttress of the Yokum Ridge. Both climbers were struck by rocks. One had a severely swollen hand which was not broken. The other had a more serious hip injury. The two were initially able to continue, each under his own power, to a previously identified safe area. At that point the climber suffering a hip injury could not continue due to excessive shock. The two climbers assessed their situation, hoping that they could stabilize the injuries enough to descend Cathedral Ridge to Lolo Pass Road on their own. By 1230 they realized and accepted that a rescue would be necessary. They attempted to call for help on their VHF radio using the state SAR frequency, but were unsuccessful. They then scanned the channels on their Sport Radios and found they could receive a number of conversations on channels 1 and 2. They called for assistance on Channel 1 and received a response from Mike Wold who had been summoned by his sons, Fletcher and Parker, when they heard the call for assistance. Through Mike Wold the Clakamas County Sheriff was informed of the situation and three ground teams were called out. The Sheriff also asked the 939th rescue unit if they would accept the mission and they did. Permission was obtained from the USFS for an air evacuation from their property. At 1700 the climbers were attended to and transported by the 939th Rescue team. They were taken to Legacy Emmanuel Hospital in Portland. As of Wednesday evening, June 21, both climbers had been released from the hospital and were able to return home without assistance.
Analysis
The Sandy Glacier Headwall route is on the west side of Mount Hood. It is not a frequently climbed route due largely to its distance from any trailheads.

Iain and Jim followed the typical approach, which is to climb up from Timberline Lodge on the south side to Illumination Saddle, then cross the Reid Glacier to Yokum Ridge. Like most routes on Mount Hood, this one relies on snow for travel. It is an alpine climbing, or mountaineering, route. It is not a hike, nor is it a rock climb. The descent is typically down the south side route.

The freezing level had been low recently but was rising at the time. The snow was refrozen enough to travel on comfortably with crampons. Snow cover on the route was good and only a very small section of the traverse around Yokum Ridge was bare. The headwall above the Sandy Glacier which constitutes the main climb to the summit ridges appeared to have very good snow coverage. The climbers saw a couple if isolated rocks fall as they approached the Sandy Glacier, but not more than one at a time and not an amount that is unusual for the Oregon Cascades. The pair spent all day Wednesday on the Sandy Glacier and did not observe any further large rockfall events, even in the heat of the afternoon.

The length of time the climbers took to assess their injuries—five hours—would have delayed the rescue significantly if airlift resources had not been available. Ground teams would have had to proceed in darkness.

For this route, a cellular phone would be a better choice for alerting authorities. Iain Morris believes that his helmet saved his life. (Sources: Oregon Mountaineering Association and Jeff Scheetz)

FALL ON ICE, ANCHOR AND CARABINER PROBABLY FAILED
Pennsylvania, Kitnersville, The Main Flow

About noon on December 27, JW (43) and BA (36) started on an ice climb popularly know as "The Banana" (WI 4) but more correctly called "The Main Flow" in Kitnersville. The conditions were good that day—cold (25-28 degrees F), cloudy, with somewhat brittle ice. The pair climbed the first 200 feet of the climb in two pitches with JW, the more experienced, leading. At this point they lowered a rope to a third climber BM (42) who had just arrived and wished to join them for the final pitch. All three men had been on the route before with JW having the most ascents. The crux second pitch having been completed, JW started on the longer final pitch (WI 3). While BM belayed from the trees to the right of the climb, BA sharpened a tool with a broken tip.

On the 70-80- degree ramp portion of the third pitch, JW placed ice screws at 28 feet and about 47 feet from the icy ledge at the base of the pitch and slightly above the belay. JW clipped both of the 8.8mm Bluewater ropes that they used into these pieces. His third screw, about 65 feet up on a 90-degree section, only got one rope since it was in better ice about five to six feet left of the line of the climb. At the top of the vertical section, at about 77 feet, JW put in a fourth screw and attached both ropes. At this point the climb gains a small ledge, taking the leader out of view of the belayer. Following this is a 12-foot vertical section. Down into the top of this formation JW placed his fifth and final screw at about 89 feet. The climb then angles slightly left on easy stepped terrain with some vertical sections of five feet or less. It ends at a rappel station on trees at about 157 feet from the base.

JW was out of sight and well above his last piece when he fell. There was no warning for the fall, no scream. Five or six feet of rope that came back to the belay was seen falling. He hit several times on the way down. His fall was to the left of his gear. With rope stretch, JW hit the icy ledge slightly above the belay head-first at a 60-70-degree angle.

The rescue call went in for help at about 2:00 p.m. The rescuers were on the scene very quickly. The Upper Black Eddy Fire Co., the Riegelsville-Palisades Fire Co., and the Point Pleasant High Angle Rescue Team among those responding. Almost as soon as the first rescue vehicles appeared on Route 32 at the base of the climb, there were three Philadelphia area news helicopters flying overhead. The noise of these helicopters made it extremely difficult for BA on the cliff with JW to communicate with the rescuers below and above. BM had informed the rescuers that there were houses on the top and that the best access would be from above. They lacked ascenders to use the rope BM had rappelled down on. The Point Pleasant Team set up on top of the cliff to get a Stokes basket down to JW. BA brought up blankets to keep JW warm and set a two-ice-screw anchor near JW's head for future use.

BM figured out that an EMT could gain the ledge quickly if he was belayed up a less icy rock corner to the right of the flow. The EMT from the Riegelsville-Pallisades Fire Co. had a little rock climbing experience and no crampons or ice tools for the climb. BA used one of the climbing ropes and slings to rig a new belay on trees. BA again had great difficulty hearing or being heard over the helicopters. The EMT climbed to within 30 feet of the ledge, but the icy cracks in a vertical section proved too difficult for further progress. BA inquired about the possibility of the use of Prusiks to finish the ascent. BA dropped slings down to be used in this manner, but it quickly became evident that the EMT lacked the experience to use them and that BA would not be able to explain how to Prusik over the din of the helicopters. Instead BA fixed the free end of the rope to the belay and then tied loops in the rope so that the EMT would have a rope ladder to climb while BA continued to belay. From there the EMT was belayed to JW's position. As the EMT made his initial assessments BA hauled up his medical bag. The EMT intubated JW to keep his airway open, fitted JW with a neck collar and radioed his condition to those below.

The Point-Pleasant High Angle Rescue Team is a group of volunteers that mainly respond to incidents at Ralph Stover State Park—a popular nearby rock climbing area. They responded very quickly and bravely especially considering their lack of ice climbing gear or experience, plus they were less familiar with these cliffs. During this time the Point-Pleasant Team was trying to reach the ledge from above. When BA saw that the red rope they had lowered had reached the ledge, he shouted to let them know that they could start down. These shouts again were drowned out by the helicopters, because several minutes later BA heard them asking over the EMT's radio if rescuers below could verify that their rope had reached the ledge. BA then asked the EMT to relay this information to the team above with his radio. The Point-Pleasant Team then started down the rope to the ledge. About this time BM came back up to the ledge using Prussiks.

The Kitnersville cliffs are poorly bonded and friable red shale. They gain co-hesion with the winter freeze so that ice climbing is safe. Nevertheless there is still a lot of loose rock to knock down in addition to hanging ice. Rappelling must be done with delicacy to reduce these dangers, especially in less traveled areas. As the first two members of the Point-Pleasant Team rappelled to the ledge, they knocked a few small rocks down. As a third member came down the rope, BA thought to warn him about the loose rock. His shouts were again fu-tile even at a distance of 50 feet due to the din of the helicopters. Not 10 feet further down the rope, the rappeller knocked at least 100 pounds of rock down. Fortunately no one was injured, but it hit close to the six people on the ledge and continued on to the ground where most of the personnel were located. BA and BM screamed warnings of "Rock!" but these too were probably lost in the noise. That these rescuers suffered increased risks just so someone could get a better camera angle seems particularly odious.

A difficult litter lower was completed, taking about three hours, and JW was flown to St. Luke's Hospital in Bethlehem, PA. He died the next day from his injuries and probably would have done so even with instantaneous help.

Analysis

The gear was retrieved two days after the accident after a half-inch of new ice had formed over it. The measurements were taken eight days after the fall and are based on memory of the placements so they are not totally accurate. The climb had changed considerably in the meantime and 12 inches of snow had fallen. It is thus conceivable that JW was at the rappel station when he fell, since there is only a three-foot difference between the rappel station at 157 feet and the calculated fall of 154 feet. Also BM, the belayer, recalled that no rope had gone out for a short time preceding the fall.

On recovery of the gear it was learned that the fifth screw at 89 feet was missing the carabiner that would have attached to the ropes. This fifth screw showed no signs of impact and BM does not remember any significant tug or jerk before the fourth screw caught the fall. The carabiner on the fourth screw was deeply notched by the impact. The screw eye also was slightly bent.

Additional thoughts on what might have happened to the rope-side carabiner on the fifth screw: 1) It came off the sling and was on the ropes and went unnoticed. Certainly this was possible given the chaos that ensued, but it is not what was remembered. 2) It broke and we have not found the pieces. This is possible only if it could happen without marking the carabiner at the screw and without a noticed jerk at the belay. There was a lip, but no sharp edges nearby. Chris Harmston of Black Diamond performed an analysis of the situation based on accounts, diagrams, and video of the area. His analysis points to carabiner failure as the most likely cause. 3) It might have come off both ropes and the sling through vibration, but this seems unlikely.

As for what initiated the fall, this will never be known. Evidence suggests that JW was at the rappel station, but not fully anchored to it. Something then happened to make this anchor fail. Obviously another piece of gear could have lessened the severity of his fall. JW was on easy ground for him (he has climbed WI 6) and may have been unaware of how far he was above his last piece. He did not have any more screws with him to place, but he did still have a Spectre or could have slung a small tree with some effort. As for the fifth screw, perhaps a locking carabiner or two in opposition would have been better before such a long run out.

Some notes on the media involvement in the story. The noise generated by three news helicopters was overwhelming on a cliff where communication is difficult if one car goes by on the road below. Their noise made it extremely difficult for BA and BM to talk to each other and to talk to the rescuers. They significantly increased the risks, while slowing the response of those involved. For JW, BA, BM and most climbers to have a rescuer killed or injured attempting their rescue provides a greater fear than their own injury or death. To have these generous people harassed and endangered for a news story seems irresponsible at best and possibly criminal. The value of this story was pure spectacle. The people that needed to know the information, JW's family and friends, would have been much better served by a caring phone call. Instead the story only created panic, as all the ice climbers in the area got frantic phone calls from friends and loved ones to see if it was them on the cliff. The story certainly did not warrant nor need live helicopter "dramatic footage" from the scene.

The media continued to behave poorly after they left the rescue. They failed to report the noise of the helicopters as a problem for the rescue even though BA made pointed remarks about it in a statement given as he left the incident. Reporters then had to be kept at bay by the hospital staff from the family and friends who came to visit. When approached for footage shot from the helicopters to assist in the investigation of why the gear failed, they flatly refused saying they would only turn over the part shown on TV and not without "a court order." Finally Yvonne Latty, a reporter from the Philadelphia *Daily News* approached the family to do a story about the incident. BA and BM gave her an extensive interview including taking her to the scene so that she could get photos as well as an idea of the dangers of the area and the difficulties of communication. She did not include anything about the helicopters causing problems, indicating that the Rescue Captain had said they were not a problem. We requested that she include the addresses of the rescue squads that JW's family and friends have sent money to. The article that did come out only sensationalized the sport and used JW's death to highlight the dangers. (Source: BA - who asked that we only use initials)

FALL FROM ROCK WHILE SETTING UP RAPPEL, NO HELMET
Tennessee, Prentice Cooper State Park
On May 1, Chris Chesnutt (30) and two friends, Jerry Roberts (34) and Travis Eisman (30) spent a long day climbing in an undeveloped area in Prentice Cooper State Park (just west of Chattanooga). Following the completion of a new route they named Ironic (5.11), Chris moved away from the cliff edge and, feeling comfortable with his position, untied from the rope and began setting up a rappel. As Chris reported, "It was getting dark fast and I wanted to get back to camp before darkness fell. In the process of setting up the rappel, I

apparently mis-stepped and fell backward 80 feet to rocks below." Chris sustained multiple injuries, including a fracture to the upper face and mandible and fracture to both feet (right calcaneous, closed fracture of the left calcaneous and talus), a fractured left arm (both radius and humerus), a compression fracture of C-5 vertebrae, and a pelvic fracture. He was not wearing a helmet.

Analysis

I believe the combination of low light, exhaustion, and hurriedness contributed to my misjudging the security of my stance. In that situation remaining tied in to a tree or some other anchor would have prevented the fall". (Source: Chris Chesnutt)

(Editor's Note: Living to tell this story was a minor miracle. The medical and rescue report on this incident was most interesting. There was one other report from Tennessee. There were few details, but it involved a fall from rock at Foster Falls State Park, resulting in a fractured arm and leg. We know there is a lot of climbing going on at both these parks, so we need some reliable reporting.)

LOSS OF CONTROL—VOLUNTARY GLISSADE, FAULTY USE OF CRAMPONS
FALL ON SNOW, FATIGUE
Utah, Mount Olympus, North Face

The previous year we (Michael and Jane Feldhaus, 33 and 31), along with Paul (41) and Marion (36), had completed the same route on Mount Olympus in approximately 12 hours. We had decided to pursue the same route that Sunday morning of May 14. Leaving the parking area for Neffs Canyon at 7:30 a.m. would allow sufficient time to complete the route before dark. The route follows a gentle approach to the Great Couloir, which at this time of year is generally filled with snow and requires crampons and ice axes to safely climb the icy snow. The couloir opens up onto the face where some easy mountaineering scrambles and crampons and mountain axes allow access of the summit ridge west of the North Summit of Olympus. Some areas before reaching the ridge during the traverse of the face require some 5.6+ rock scrambling. After reaching the ridge, we walked it down to the west side of the west slabs. The route finishes up with a three-pitch rappel down the west side of the west slabs. From this point it is generally an easy walk down the snow filled gully present in front of the west slabs... but not this day.

Jane was first in the group heading down the snow gully with her crampons on and ax in hand. The snow was generally soft and slushy with intermittent icy spots at this late hour in the day, 8:30 p.m. We were about one hour (two miles) from the end of the route at this point. We were making good progress plunge-stepping down the 40-50-degree snow slope when Jane's snow-and-ice-filled crampon slipped and she started sliding down the snow on her butt. Jane was not too worried, as her forward progress was relatively slow and she felt she could easily stop. So she enjoyed the "free ride." However, as she picked up speed and was headed toward large rocks, she rolled over to self-arrest and immediately dislocated her shoulder. But she was still able to arrest. She knew immediately her shoulder was dislocated. Mike quickly started getting more clothing on her as she already looked "shocky." Within minutes Paul and Marion were on the scene. A quick conference in the group lead us to send Paul out to call for a mountain rescue as no one in the group felt comfortable reducing her shoulder. At this point the sun had set and a stiff breeze was coming down the gully. The snow was now returning to a hard ice. Marion, Mike, and Jane immobilized Jane's shoulder by placing a one-liter nalgene water bottle in her armpit and immobilized her arm with some extra webbing. We also put on all available extra clothing from our packs. We then started to move her down the 400 meters of ice and snow. The technique we used to move Jane down the snow was to empty her pack and put the pack in a garbage bag. She then sat on the pack to help insulate her from the snow. With two mountain axes plunged in the snow just below her feet we were able to gently move her down the snow field by alternating the removal and placement of each ax one to two feet lower. This allowed her to remain secure with one ax used as a foot stop and allow her to slide down to the next ax stop. There was a rock shelf at the edge of the snowfield approximately 200 meters down from the fall. We made it to the ledge to rest and wait for help. By this point Jane was almost doubled over in pain from the muscle spasms in her shoulder, neck, and back. To take her mind off of it and to stay warm, we decided to continue down the snow field using the same method used earlier. As we moved her out to sit down on the pack once again, the jostling, the water bottle and good luck allowed her shoulder to reduce itself. At approximately 11:30 p.m., the first of 30 rescuers from the Salt Lake County Sheriff's Mountain Rescue Squad arrived. We were approximately 40 yards from the end of the snowfield and continued down to the end of it. After a quick assessment of Jane's condition, the mountain rescuers loaded her into a Stokes litter, lowered her down some rock falls, and carried her out. (Source: Michael and Jane Feldhaus)

Analysis

There were two major factors that led to this accident. There was overall fatigue of the group that led to the misstep and subsequent fall on the soft snow. She would not have gathered as much speed and therefore may not have had the stresses on her shoulder that lead to the dislocation. The second factor may have been that her muscles were very tired and she may not have been in the best position when her ax caught and stopped her fall. A third factor was that her crampons, while okay to have on as long as she was not glissading, filled with snow. Finally, no one in the group had backcountry first aid experience, let alone knowledge of how to reduce a dislocated shoulder. Had we been able to reduce her shoulder immediately, the shoulder would have recovered faster with less damage and the group may have been able to slowly and safely move out of the backcountry without assistance.

By the time we reached Jane Feldhaus, her shoulder had self-reduced, but she was still in pain and unable to walk out. She was immobilized in a bean-bag vacuum splint in the litter, lowered about 15 pitches down the Z-couloir of Mount Olympus and then wheeled down the Z-trail to the road. (Source: Victims and Tom Moyer - Salt Lake County Sheriff's SAR)

FALL ON ROCK—INADEQUATE BELAY WHILE LOWERING
Utah, American Forks Canyon, Rockapella

On June 1, Aaron Johnson (17) was being lowered from Rockappella, but his partner could not hold him. The rope started pulling her up. Another young woman grabbed on to her, but even the two of them could not hold his weight. They let go. Johnson fell 25 feet straight to the ground, suffering back and neck injuries. (Source: Dennis Chapman - Utah County Sheriff's SAR)

Analysis

Obviously there was a considerable weight discrepancy between climber and belayer. It is common practice to be adequately anchored when belaying, whether one's partner is climbing or being lowered. (Source: Jed Williamson)

FALL ON ROCK—LOWERING ERROR, INADEQUATE PROTECTION, NO HARD HAT, EXCEEDING ABILITIES
Utah, Parley's Canyon, Salt Lake City

On June 17, CH (19), DK (19), and LH (19) were climbing in Parley's Canyon, Salt Lake City. DK was preparing to climb, belayed by CH at the top of the route, but appeared to be having trouble tying into the rope. Another climber, waiting to climb the route, assisted him in tying in. The climbers watched DK successfully climb the route. They then saw CH appear over the top as if he were going to be lowered. Instead, he fell about 80 feet to the base of the crag with the rope attached.

When SAR team members arrived, CH was conscious, but suffering from a femur fracture and two ankle fractures. He was immobilized in a bean-bag vacuum splint and lowered one pitch down a steep scree slope to the road, then flown by Lifeflight helicopter to the hospital.

Analysis

After DK completed the climb, he exchanged positions with CH and prepared to lower him. When he started to lower, the rope ran through his hands, burning them. He was forced to let go in order to avoid being pulled over the edge himself.

The rope ran from CH, through slings attached to a two-bolt anchor, to a tubular belay device attached to DK's harness. He was positioned above the anchor, and was not tied in. When asked to show how he had rigged the belay device, he threaded it correctly, but appeared unsure as to which side of the rope to hold. It appears likely that he had been holding the climber's side of the rope. Even if he held the correct side of the rope, he would likely have been pulled off his stance as he began to lower. This also could have caused him to let go of the rope.

The setup described is commonly used for top roping when the belayer is on the ground. When the belay is done from the top of the climb, the belayer should tie in. Ideally, the belayer should be located at or below the anchor. When this is not possible, belaying should only be done from a solid stance, preferably seated with the feet braced. (Source: Tom Moyer - Salt Lake County Sheriff's SAR)

FALL ON ROCK–RAPPEL ERROR, DARKNESS
Utah, Zion National Park, Grasshopper

On October 8, Eric Wehrly (33) and his partner Ian Whyte were rappelling the final 80 feet from the climb named Grasshopper when this incident occurred. Wehrly was the first one down. He set up the rappel by doubling his rope—but not exactly. One end was short by 20 feet, and that is the distance he fell to the cliff bottom. He proceeded to roll and tumble another two to three feet until finally coming to a stop.

Whyte was able to get down to the road and flag down the Zion shuttle bus. Fortunately, the Zion Park ambulance and personnel were able to respond quickly, treating and transporting Wehrly to a helicopter. He was taken to Las Vegas University Medical Trauma Center.

He sustained multiple system traumatic injuries, including a severe head injury, flail chest, bilateral fractured clavicles, and a pneumothorax. (Source: Cindy Purcell, NPS Ranger, Zion National Park)

Analysis

Perhaps fatigue played a part here, as these were two experienced climbers. That Wehrly did not at least tie individual knots in the ends of the doubled rope is surprising. It would have been even better to have tied the ends together before tossing them down. Hopefully there will come a year when this kind of incident does not happen. (Source: Jed Williamson)

FALL ON ICE, CLIMBING ALONE, PLACED NO PROTECTION
Utah, Provo Canyon, Stairway to Heaven

On December 18, a man (24) was on the second pitch of Stairway to Heaven when he fell attempting to climb over an ice bulge. Both feet popped from their holds. He dropped 50 feet to the ground, suffering a compression fracture of L-5. (Source: Dennis Chapman - Utah County Sheriff's SAR)

STRANDED, FALL ON ROCK, PROTECTION PULLED
Virginia, Seneca Rocks

In early April, a climber (age unknown) started soloing a chimney on the West Face of the North Peak. He got up 15 or 20 feet and decided that he would rather have a rope, so his partner threw the end of the rope up to him and the climber tied in. He placed a Camalot, climbed a few feet farther, and then fell. The Camalot pulled. The climber fell down the chimney, sustaining severe head and internal injuries. He was unconscious when several climbers with EMT training first reached him They unsuccessfully tried CPR to resuscitate him when his heart stopped. (He was not wearing a helmet, though later comments from the coroner indicated that a helmet probably would not have saved him due to the severity of internal injuries.)

Analysis

For me, the most import lesson from this accident came a month later, when I heard via the Internet that the victim had tested positive for Hepatitis B. While one of the ambulance crew had asked the police personnel present at the accident to record the name and phone number of those who assisted in the recovery effort, it turned out that only about half of those involved had been recorded. As a result, many of these people (myself included) who had significant contact with the victim's blood did not learn about the lab test until long after the time period during which a prophylactic treatment for Hepatitis B is useful—typically 7 to 10 days after contact. Fortunately, it was later discovered that the initial test results were incorrect.

If you are involved in a rescue, make sure you find out who you can contact to get any medical information that may be relevant to rescuers, and follow it up. Climbers often have many nicks and cuts on their hands after a day of climbing, and in this age of serious blood-borne diseases it is a good idea to carry a pair of latex gloves and some prepackaged handi-wipes in the event you assist in a rescue or recovery. (Source: Chris Leger)

(Editor's Note: Latex gloves are standard items for even the smallest of First Aid Kits. On the other hand, First Aid Kits do not yet seem to be a standard item carried by climbers. At places like Seneca, the Gunks, Joshua Tree, etc., day packs are often left on the ground. Having a FAK in them is a good idea.)

FALLING SNOW/ICE–CORNICE COLLAPSE
Washington, Mount Rainier, Panorama Point

On April 30, Rainier Mountaineering, Inc., was conducting the second day of their annual guide tryouts. There were 52 applicants and about 15 RMI guides who had hiked to the Panorama Point area to conduct training/evaluation. About the 6800-foot level, the group took a break to rest, put on additional clothing, and awaited the next phase of the tryouts. While they were resting, guides Pete Whittaker and Paul Maier began to scout the area that they refer to as "Upper Cornice." They were evaluating a route which would lead the group safely past the cornice to their standard training area toward Golden Gate. It was determined that the group could safely pass well to the west of the cornice and descend around the southern end of the cornice. This would allow the guides to evaluate the applicants' descent skills as well as lead them into the traditional training area using what appeared to be a safe route. Whittaker and Maier then rejoined the group and Whittaker met with the other guides to start dividing the applicants into smaller groups. Maier, Cate Casson (c.34) and John Lucia returned toward the cornice to further explore and kick in a descent route. As Maier got lower and could see the underside of the cornice, he could tell that it was dangerously overhung, so he shouted to the other guides to stay on his tracks or to the west of them. He also placed a ski pole to act as a marker and further instructed the other guides to stay to the west of his pole. Within 30 seconds or so after warning the others of the overhang, the cornice collapsed. Maier stated that it ran from where he stood about 150 feet, all the way to its northern end. In the debris he could see Casson lying on her back. Maier shouted to Casson to determine her condition, and she replied that she thought she might have a broken back. At this point, Whittaker assumed the role of site commander and sent guides to Paradise to get medical gear. Several other guides attended to Casson's injuries. When the backboard and litter arrived, Casson was stabilized and placed in the litter and then transported to Paradise through Edith Creek Basin.

According to Cate Casson's account, she was in the middle of the cornice about 30 yards to the west of the lip when she began to scout. She began to angle toward the edge and got within 30 feet of the lip when she began to parallel the cornice. At the closest point to the lip, Casson estimated that she was about 20 feet from the edge. She began to travel west away from the lip when she heard a loud "pop" and saw a crack open up under her feet. She fell backwards and was pinched together by two large blocks of snow as she fell. She landed on her back. Her estimate of the fall distance was approximately 20 vertical feet. She tried to move her legs, but could not, so she waited for the other guides to effect her rescue.

Paul Maier yelled up to Peter Whittaker that Cate had fallen with the cornice and was now visible within the blocks at the base. Peter instructed Paul to get a head count of the guides and put RMI supervisor George Dunn in charge of the applicants. George immediately took the applicants away from the accident site, chose three or four guides to help him, and sent all other guides to the accident site for assistance. An avalanche guard was posted above the cornice and once initial medical information regarding Cate's status was relayed, Peter communicated via radio and cell phone to NPS Comm center and RMI base in Ashford. RMI guides Paul Maier, Brent Okita, Brenda Walsh, and Kent Wagner attended Cate—all EMT or OEC certified. RMI guides John Lucia, Matt Farmer, and Ben Marshall were sent to Paradise to locate and bring back oxygen, backboard, trauma pack, and sled. While waiting for medical supplies, Cate was treated for shock and suspected lower body, crushing injuries. Vitals were taken systematically. Upon arrival of medical equipment, Cate was secured to the backboard with a cervical collar and then placed into a sled. Evacuation from the accident site to Paradise was via Edith Creek Basin.

In a follow-up call to RMI, it was learned that Casson had suffered fractures to the L-1 and L-2 vertebrae, and although she was expected to make a full recovery, she would be in a body cast for several months and then need to undergo extensive physical rehabilitation. (Source: Rick Kirchner, NPS Ranger, Mount Rainier National Park)

FALLING ICE, NO HARD HAT
Washington, Mount Rainier, Ingraham Glacier
On June 4, an ice fall occurred from the top of an 80- to 100-oot ice cliff that the climbing route crosses underneath. In the path were Rainier Mountaineering, Inc., guides and clients. The ice broke apart and spread rapidly, gaining speed. It was dark at the time, and thus difficult to see what was coming down— and where. Two climbers, both guides, were seriously injured, including facial laceration and head trauma. They were able to walk back to Camp Muir, but needed to be evacuated by helicopter from there.

Three others were injured but were able to walk out. (Source: From a Mount Rainier Case Incident Report)

LOSS OF CONTROL—VOLUNTARY GLISSADE, FALL ON SNOW, HIT AND DRAGGED BY FALLING CLIMBER, INEXPERIENCE, MISPERCEPTION
Washington, Silver/Tinkham Peaks

On June 8, Joe Myers (40), Jacob Engelstein (40), and Phil Loe (58) were attempting to climb Tinkham Peak, an easy, non-technical climb. The route was snow-covered above 4,400 feet. Owing to poor visibility, the climb was aborted at 4,900 feet. The party descended to just above 4,400 feet, where Myers glissaded only a few feet when he discovered an ice crust below an inch or two of snow. He attempted to arrest, but struck a tree. A few seconds later, Engelstein fell and struck Loe. Losing his ice ax on 45-degree snow, Engelstein panicked and seized Loe's right foot with both hands. Loe, now sliding head-first on his back—still gripped by Engelstein—struck a tree. Both came to an abrupt stop. Aid was summoned by cell phone. A 10-hour litter carry ensued.

Loe was diagnosed with a comminuted fracture of the distal femur. Myers sustained a fractured rib.

Analysis

Engelstein and Myers were inexperienced, having been instructed in ice ax use just two months earlier. Although beginning climbers may appear to be strong and able, one needs to keep a close eye on them. Belaying the two beginners would have prevented the injuries, but the terrain was such that no one would have seen a need to belay. (Source: Phil Loe)

FROSTBITE—WEATHER CONDITIONS, FAILURE TO TURN BACK, FALLS ON SNOW AND INTO CREVASSES
Washington, Mount Rainier, Kautz Glacier

On June 9 at 1700, David German and his partner Judy Rittenhouse left their high camp at 10,200 feet on the Wapowety Cleaver in an attempt to climb the Kautz Glacier Route. The party found themselves encountering increasingly poor weather. For some reason, the party continued to ascend to the summit in whiteout conditions, wanding their route. Upon descending, German attempted to follow his wands but took a 10-foot fall into an open crevasse which pulled Rittenhouse off her feet and down 50 feet. Both were able to walk out. Continuing on, the two wandered off their wanded course and unknowingly began to descend the Wilson Headwall. German then fell into another open crevasse. Rittenhouse attempted to arrest the fall, but was unable to do so. The force of the fall slingshoted Rittenhouse over the crevasse to the lower side before she was able to arrest. German then climbed out. At this point the team decided to dig a snow cave and bivy (at 13,000 feet). On June 10 the party attempted to descend further in poor conditions (whiteout, high winds and soft snow). After two hours the team, unable to determine their location, decided to dig in again, excavating a new snow cave.

June 11 brought continued severe weather and poor traveling conditions, keeping the two holed up in their snow cave. On June 12 the visibility improved enough to allow German and Rittenhouse to determine their location (upper reaches of the Wilson Headwall), but they delayed descent until the following day.

On June 13 at 0800, weak and dehydrated, they slowly descended and crossed the Kautz following their wands. At 1430 the party returned to their high camp (after a few more "minor" crevasse falls) to find their tent badly ripped and full of snow, tent poles broken. Seeing another party below, they descended to their camp at 9,340 feet to seek assistance. The Reike-Crank Rainier party assisted the German party. The German party reestablished camp next to them.

On June 14, German awoke with acutely painful feet which was self-diagnosed as frostbite. Later in the day, believing himself unable to walk out, German asked for assistance from the NPS relaying his request through the Crank Rainier party using "talk-about" radios to communicate with a party member at Paradise. At 1530, Climbing Ranger Glenn Kessler arrived at Paradise and was told of the situation by Paul Soboleski, a base coordinator for the Crank Rainier party. By radio, Kessler and Soboleski contacted the parties at 9,350 feet. German relayed that he was unable to walk and requested assistance. Kessler explained that due to very high avalanche danger and poor weather, assistance would be delayed until conditions permitted. Kessler then arranged for a medical evaluation of German to be performed by a nurse with the Crank Rainier party. At 1830, the medical evaluation showed some frostbite signs on both feet. Most of the injury appeared superficial to the nurse, except for a two-centimeter-in-diameter portion on the right big toe, and a one-centimeter-portion on the smallest digit, which appeared very dark in color. In the opinion of the nurse, German should be able to walk off. German and Rittenhouse agreed that he would be able to walk, but requested assistance for the descent from camp.

NPS Ranger Steve Winslow was apprised of the circumstances by Kessler. After a thorough discussion of options, Winslow determined that the most appropriate course of action was to prepare for an assist the following morning if conditions allowed. Kessler began a call-out of available Climbing Rangers.

At 0600 on June 15, Kessler was joined by Rangers Jennifer Erxleben (VIP) and Paul Charleton, along with Crank Rainier's Paul Soboleski at the Paradise Old Station. Gear from the Longmire SAR cache and Paradise SAR cache was assembled. At 0630, Uwe Nehring, Incident Commander, contacted Kessler at Paradise. It was agreed that a consultation with a doctor should be made prior to asking the German party to move. The resulting medical opinion was that German should be removed from the field as soon as conditions would allow and that avoidance of further damage from walking would be beneficial. Kessler then apprised the German party of this information and that greater assistance would be available. Helicopter LZ suitability was discussed with those on the scene. German, however, relayed that he wanted to begin walking down and refused additional help beyond a ground team to carry his gear. IC was apprised of the circumstances and the ground assist was set in motion. Additional overnight provisions, avalanche rescue gear and glacier travel gear was collected. At 0730, Rangers were notified that the German party had begun their descent. Rangers Stoney Richards (VIP) and Matt Hendrickson joined Kessler, Erxleben and Charleton, and the "assist" team left Paradise at 0800. At the time of the departure, visibility was poor, with light drizzle and very light winds.

Due to recent avalanche activity elsewhere on the mountain, an avalanche pit was dug above Glacier Vista and avalanche conditions were assessed to be relatively stable for slopes of similar aspect and elevation. The team then proceeded downhill below the moraine alongside the Nisqually Glacier. While gearing up for glacier travel, the visibility began to improve and a party of four followed by a party of two was witnessed crossing the Nisqually Glacier below the "Fan." When the party of four reached the Rangers, it was confirmed that the following party was the German party. When the German party reached the Rangers, they appeared to be traveling at a reasonable pace and were in good spirits. Rangers took the contents out of German's pack to carry down to Paradise. The German party was assisted back to the Paradise Old Station where a detailed report of the incident was obtained. Medial evaluations were refused; however, the patients both signed EMS release forms. The German party indicated that they would seek further medical evaluation at Harborview Hospital in Seattle and report back the results of their evaluations to the Old Station by phone. (Source: Report prepared by Glenn Kessler and Jennifer Erxleben, NPS Rangers, Mount Rainier National Park)

Analysis

David German wrote a report describing the details found above. He indicated that on the ascent, when they had reached the Wilson Headwall and Fuhrer Finger, Judy "suggested that we turn back." By the time they reached the crater rim, it was a complete whiteout. "Judy again suggested turning back, but the summit was so close!" His concluding statement was this: "We had survived. Poor judgment cost us dearly, but competent mountaineering skills (and some luck) brought us back alive (barely). Skills and technical competence are requirements for mountaineering, but nothing will ever substitute for good judgment." (Source: Jed Williamson)

FALL INTO CREVASSE, CLIMBING UNROPED, OFF ROUTE
Washington, Mount Rainier, Interglacier

On July 22, Thomas Porro (41) fell into a crevasse on the Interglacier. He was traveling with a partner, Mike Spillane, but they were not roped. Porro said he saw a snow bridge and crevasse on each side, but decided not to follow the trail around the crevasse. The bridge collapsed while he was crossing. He fell at least 50 feet to a ledge. He believes his pack saved his life by breaking the fall. His partner lowered a rope and Porro was able to tie in before hypothermia and shock reduced his mobility.

Rangers effected a rescue. They found that Mr. Porro had a fractured right foot, sprained left knee, and a contusion and laceration of the right eye orbit. He was extricated from the crevasse, then helicoptered from the mountain. (Source: David Orsatti, NPS Ranger, Mount Ranier National Park)

FALLING ROCK
Washington, Mt. Rainier, Kautz Cleaver.

On the evening of July 24, Rainier National Park rescuers, aided by an Army Reserve Chinook helicopter, rescued Tony Leak (47) from the 12,200-foot level of Kautz Cleaver on Mount Rainier. Leak and his two sons Joshua (17) and Caleb (15) were climbing on Kautz Cleaver and had stopped to camp. Leak had removed his climbing helmet to set up camp when spontaneous rock-fall struck the trio. Mr. Leak sustained head injuries. One of Leak's sons called 911 on a cellular phone and was connected to Climbing Rangers at Camp Muir.

A Ranger team on the summit was dispatched to the site and reached the Leak's after considerable effort. A Ranger/EMT, assisted by doctors through a radio and phone link to a local hospital, assessed Leak's condition and determined that it was more serious than anyone originally thought. Equipment and additional rescuers were lowered to the scene by the Chinook. Leak was hoisted to the helicopter after being lowered by sled to the landing zone and flown to Madigan Army Medical Center for treatment. (Source: Steve Winslow, NPS Ranger, Mount Ranier National Park)

Analysis

"People think this was a climbing accident, but actually the mountain just cut loose and dumped on me as I was getting ready for bed," Leak said from his room at Madigan Army Medical Center. He was in stable condition recovering from a broken neck, back and head injuries.

Caleb, who has been climbing with his father for about four years, said the harrowing trip brought the family together. "It was kind of rough at times. But it was well worth it," he told *The Seattle Times*. Leak said he owes his condition today to the boys' first-aid assistance.

(Editor's Note: There was a considerable amount of cell phone conversation involved in this incident. The rangers called Mr. Leak's wife. She had received calls from her husband and sons. She informed the Rangers that she did not think the boys could be of help, given their level of experience. Initially, Mr. Leak told the Rangers he thought he could descend without assistance, but this did not prove to be the case.)

HAPE
Washington, Mount Rainier, Fuhrer's Finger

Tim Hartman contacted Mount Rainier National Park at 7:08 a.m. on August 12 to report that his partner Neil Shriner (41) was very ill. Shriner's symptoms included difficulty breathing, gurgling lung sounds, and dizziness when standing. Hartman and Shriner had climbed to 12,000 feet on the Fuhrer Finger route the previous day, setting up their camp when Shriner started to feel sick. His condition deteriorated during the night. Hartman believed that his partner was suffering from High Altitude Pulmonary Edema and that they would need a rescue, as Shriner was unable to move safely.

A helicopter rescue was effected by park rangers by 3:30 p.m. At Madigan Hospital, he was diagnosed with HAPE. (Source: Mike Gauthier, SAR Ranger, Mount Ranier National Park)

Analysis

This report is included to remind us that High Altitude Pulmonary Edema can come on quickly, even at moderate altitude. (Source: Jed Williamson)

FALL ON SNOW, FAULTY USE OF CRAMPONS
Washington, North Cascades National Park, Mount Shuksan, Fisher Chimneys Route

On September 16, John Nedila (50) slipped on a 50-degree snow slope on the Fisher Chimneys route on Mount Shuksan. He slid about 125 feet to rocks below, suffering injuries to his face, torso, and extremities. He was wearing crampons at the time.

Two passersby rendered aid. Nedila was semiconscious at first and complained of an ache in his side. But he lost both consciousness and pulse within 15 minutes. CPR was administered for 20 minutes without effect.

Rangers were unable to recover the body until the next day. (Source: Alan Budahl, Outdoor Network)

VARIOUS FALLS ON ROCK, PROTECTION PROBLEMS (3), HAND STUCK IN HOLD
Wisconsin, Baraboo State Park

Four reports came in from Baraboo State Park this year. All involved leader falls and three resulted in fractures. One resulted in a dislocation when the leader's hand got stuck in a hold as he fell. One fall involved a man going back up unroped to retrieve a piece of protection 30 feet up. He fell as he was reaching for the piece. The other two involved protection coming out and a belay anchor coming away.

The reports are sketchy, so not much can be gleaned other than the fact that protection placement and anchoring are still problems here. (Source: From Case Incident Reports received from Baraboo State Park)

FALL ON SNOW—BACK COUNTRY SKIING, TRAVELING ALONE
Wyoming, Grand Teton National Park

On April 11, Vito Seskunas (53) obtained a backcountry permit at the Moose Visitor Center for a five day ski trip to Death Canyon. He parked at the winter trailhead along the Moose-Wilson Road, and skied in. For the steeper section going up the canyon, he put climbing skins on his skis. In the afternoon, he reached where Death Canyon starts to flatten out about 300 yards below the patrol cabin. This was about five miles from his car. He skied up a gentle slope which was a drift of snow on the lee side of a boulder. When he got near the boulder, he saw that he was on a drift. He tried to ski down off the left side of the drift since trees blocked the way to the right. The left side of the drift was nearly vertical, and about 32 inches high. Below the drift, the snow was relatively level. When his ski reached the level snow, the tip dug into the snow. He heard what he assumed were breaking bones in his left ankle. His ankle was severely angulated laterally.

After the injury, Seskunas went downhill about 200 feet until he found a flat spot to set up his tent. There he spent the night. During the night he debated what to do. He had enough food and fuel to last several days, but he knew no one would miss him until the evening of April 15 at the earliest. He had not taken a cell phone since he felt they too often provided a false sense of security to backcountry travelers who should be prepared to deal with their own problems. He was without a sure way to signal for assistance. His tent was pitched on the snow covering the stream just above where it drops down the cascades leaving the flat part of the canyon. His camp had a good view of the valley from Phelps Lake to the north end of the airport and a section of the highway. He felt that if he had to stay put he could try to build a signal fire, but there was no way to know for certain that his signaling efforts were effective.

Due to the apparent severity of his injury, he decided that his highest priority was to get out so he could get medical attention as soon as possible. He became mentally very focused and compartmentalized. He refused to think about the accident or anything other than getting out.

He thought about splinting the foot, but his limited first aid training had taught him that he needed to take the boot off the foot before it was splinted. He was afraid that if he took the boot off, he would not be able to get it back on. He was concerned about keeping it as warm as possible and protected as he crawled out. He did not think about splinting over the boot and incorporating the boot into a splint using his foam chair, for example, because that was not an option presented in his first aid training. He left the boot on his injured foot as a splint.

By the morning of April 12, he had made the decision to try to get out on his own power. He felt that since he could not bear any weight on his ankle, he would go as light as possible. He took only his ski poles and some granola bars. He was dressed in a synthetic shirt and a good Gore-Tex mountain jacket on his upper body and light cotton pants with T3 ski boots. He had mitten shells and light gloves. He thought about wearing his Gore-Tex pants, but he decided not to since they had a zipper on the backside that he felt would create a pressure point. He knew that he would be sitting and sliding on his rear for a long time and he was afraid of bruising and problems from the zipper. He expected that it would take two or three days to get out.

His primary method for moving was to have his feet in front of him and to push along with his hands and pull with his good foot, with a rest on his butt while he moved his hands and foot. He followed the summer trail as best he could, even though it was covered in deep snow until he was lower in the canyon. He had to cross some steep snow fields, but they were soft enough that he was able to negotiate them with little difficulty. In general, traveling was easier when the snow was firm. Soft snow was not as easy to move through. The initial descent of Death Canyon was relatively easy compared to the flatter section from Phelps Lake Overlook to the road.

He had a good breakfast on the morning of April 12 and left camp around 0630. He stopped about 2030 that evening in the flat part of the canyon above the lake. He found a sheltering tree and made a bough bed. His pants were wet and he lay on his side to try to dry them. He was able to sleep most of the night. On occasion, he awoke with a jerk, due to muscle spasms, he thought, and then he would shiver for a few minutes. He would eventually get back to sleep, and he slept soundly from 0300 to 0600 when he wanted to get up and get moving.

When asked about the mental processes he used to keep going, he said that he loves life with a passion. He loves the outdoors and activities like climbing and skiing. The outdoors is his church. He also loves his family, friends and music. He has a lot to live for. These things provided him with a very positive image of what he did not want to lose. His life is full and he wants to experience it more. During this trip out, it never occurred to him that he might die. His mental process for getting out involved these things that are important to him. He broke the trip into mentally manageable goals using landmarks. Getting across this open space. Getting to that tree. He developed a personal mantra based on counting steps. When he moved, he counted each move. He tried to move in sets of 100 movements. He dedicated each set to someone or something he loved. He would dedicate this 100 moves to his wife, the next set to a son, the next set to his cat, etc. The numbers were important. At the end of the set, he would rest and put his hands inside his jacket to try to warm his hands in his armpits.

On the morning of April 13, he completed the flat portion at the bottom of the canyon to where the trail starts up the Phelps Lake Moraine. When he neared Phelps Lake, he thought about trying to go along the lakeshore, but the bad spring ice conditions caused him to feel that he would have to be up in the woods, and that he would likely find the going tough due to ravines and downed trees. Instead he opted to stay on the trail he used on the way in. He knew that way, and there was a chance other skiers might use the trail. Unfortunately, this was a period of poor weather that did not encourage many folks to be out. Going up over the Phelps Lake moraine was a "bear" for him. There is about 700 vertical feet that he had to gain. About two-thirds of the trail had a mound of snow on the trail tread, with the side of the trail melted out. On the third that was melted the tread was bare, and he was able to use his ski poles as crutches. This was easier for him than being on his backside. He was not able to do 100 moves without stopping while going up the moraine, but he expected that and he did as much as he could before he rested. When he neared the top, he passed a long snow slope that led down to near the lake. At that point he thought he heard voices at the lake, and for a brief moment he thought about how easy it would be to slide down the snow to seek the voices. He quickly decided that he had worked too hard to get up the moraine and that he would not think about the possibility of finding people at the lake. He passed the top of the moraine about 2030 and went another half hour before finding a tree for the night. He found the level area at the top of the overlook a challenge to determine where the trail was located and he kept going until he knew he was not straying from it.

He was able to sleep most of the night with the same irritation of being jolted awake by muscle spasms a few times. They were followed by a few minutes of shivering and then he was able to get back to sleep. He awoke at 0600 and started on again. He had hoped to get out in three days, so he was motivated to make the car by that night. The gently sloping Valley Trail was much slower going than the steeper terrain coming down the canyon. He kept to the same mantra of dedicating 100 moves to someone he loved. He passed the trailhead bulletin board at the Whitegrass cabin at 2200. He finally felt that if he kept going, he might become totally exhausted, so he stopped under a good tree at 2230. He slept well again with a few wake-ups due to cramps early in the night. He got his usual 0600 start.

On the morning of April 16 around 0900, he was met by skiers about 400 yards from his car. He asked them for food, but at first did not ask for assistance. They gave him another jacket and insulated him from the snow he was sitting on, while one of the party went to Moose to report the incident. A rescue was organized and Ranger Culver walked in as a first responder while Rangers Burgette, Page, and Spomer responded with a snowmobile, sled, and ambulance. His foot was angulated so that the leg could not be splinted with one of the usual splints. Instead, he was placed in the sled on the rescue sleeping bag, and the leg was splinted with blankets and his other leg. His legs were tied together at the knees with a triangular bandage, the top of the sleeping bag was put over him, and the straps were cinched down snug enough to stabilize him. He was then driven slowly to the trailhead.

At St. John's Hospital it was determined that his injuries included an open fracture of the left tibia, a fractured fibula, and ligament damage. His feet did not have any frostbite. Due to the blood trapped in his boot for three-and-a-half days, his injury was compounded by infection. Other injuries were minor but included abrasion of the skin on his fingers, bruised knuckles, frostnipped fingers, and extensive bruising of his backside.

Analysis

In analyzing the accident, two factors were determined to be key. The skis he was using were Rossignol Black Widows. Black Widows are noted for their stiff tips that dig into soft snow instead of flexing and riding up on top. In the afternoon, the surface of the snow was soft, and the tip dug in. Even with the tip dug in, it did not seem that there was enough energy in the fall to cause the severe open fracture/dislocation he sustained. The other key factor was the heavy pack that Seskunas was wearing. As he fell with a twisting motion with the ski relatively fixed in the snow, the weight of the pack provided the force to cause the fracture/dislocation. Skiing off the drift onto the flat snow should have been uneventful, but it was not.

Seskunas found himself in a tough situation knowing that he had a significant injury that needed attention, but knowing that no one would start looking for him until after his wife called the park when she did not hear from him on the night of April 15. He made decisions that were not necessarily the best, but he had a reason for everything he did or did not do. To do it over again, he would probably start out with his Gore-Tex pants and discard them if the zipper really became a problem. He would also probably have taken his thick Datchstein wool mittens, since the gloves and overmitts he had were trashed with the wear they received. The thicker mitts might have prevented some of the bruising on his knuckles and reduced the abrasions on the tops of his fingers.

He did not try to build fires because he was worried that with his limited mobility, if a fire got out of hand, he might not be able to move away from it quickly enough. He purposefully dressed lightly since he thought being too warm would be a bigger problem than being too cold. In fact, he was able to sleep remarkably well each night even though he was wearing a single thin layer of wet cotton on his lower body and his upper body just had a thin wicking top with a Gore-Tex shell. The weather was 20-40 degrees F, and it snowed or rained a quarter-inch of moisture on the night of April 13.

This is an example of a positive attitude, resourcefulness, the acceptance of the responsibility to take care of one's self in the backcountry and a strong will to live. (Source: Dan Burgette, SAR Coordinator, Grand Teton National Park) *(Editor's Note: While not a climbing accident, this report is included for the reasons stated in the last sentence above. I anticipate there will be some debate as to how he might have splinted his foot—and, dare I say it, whether a cell phone might have been a good idea. Those of Mr. Seskunas' generation would have done as he did, I suspect.)*

SLIP ON SNOW—TWICE, NO BELAY
Wyoming, Grand Teton National Park, Mount Moran
On July 3, the Jones party signed out at the Jenny Lake Ranger Station as two separate groups of four to climb the Skillet Glacier route on Mount Moran. On July 4, they started across Jackson Lake in two small boats headed for the base on Mount Moran. Waves swamped their boats and they were rescued by NPS Rangers. On July 5, they were delivered to the base of Moran by a Signal Mountain shuttle boat. They climbed to the Skillet moraine and camped for the night. They left camp on July 6 at 0400 in three roped teams. Four of them retreated to camp at 0700, while Ben Boykin (40), Tom Jones (43), Steve Harris and Jeb Stewart continued to the summit, arriving around 1500. (They required 11 hours for the ascent. The average time for ascent is less than seven hours.)

During the descent, Tom Jones, who was not belayed at the time and had removed his helmet, slipped and slid about 1,000 feet down the "Handle" of the Skillet. Apparently he was not injured, and after he stopped sliding, continued his descent at a more sedate pace. As he attempted to turn the "Rock Island" on the south side, he slipped again, glanced off the Rock Island, cleared the bergschrund and came to rest on the low angled section of the "Pan." The members of the party who had turned back at 0700 saw him fall and went to his assistance. They were able to get Jones back to their camp and Jim called for help on his cell phone. The call was received by the SAR coordinator at 1930.

The contract helicopter arrived at Lupine Meadows at 2015, the pilot was briefed and then transported Rangers Weathermon and Jernigan with medical equipment to a landing zone near the patient's camp. Jones was placed on a backboard and in a litter while the helicopter returned to Lupine Meadows. As the patient was moved to the landing zone, the helicopter flew back to the glacier for a pickup about 2115, arriving at Lupine Meadows at 2120. Jones was transported to St. John's Hospital by Medic 1. (Source: Tom Kimbrough, NPS Ranger, Grand Teton National Park)
Analysis
It seems inevitable to have a Skillet Glacier incident. This one was classic for

the route. Most of the slides happen on the descent. We do not know whether Jones tried—or knew how—to self-arrest. Or if he had an ice ax. No matter. Skillet Glacier on Mount Moran = pay attention. (Source: Jed Williamson)

FALL ON SNOW, CLIMBING ALONE AND UNROPED
Wyoming, Grand Teton National Park, Mount Owen

On July 15 at 1810, Rene Steque (65) fell 300 feet on snow at the base of the Koven Glacier while returning after a successful ascent of Mount Owen. He had fallen two previous times before that without injury, but on the third fall, he slid into a boulder field at the base of the snow. A. Popinchaulk, who was camped on the Teton Glacier with his son and another teenager, witnessed the fall, and immediately climbed to Steque's location to assist him. Popinchaulk rendered first aid, moved Steque out of the line of rockfall (Steque was unable to move on his own), provided him with warm clothing and a sleeping bag, secured his son and friend at their campsite on Teton Glacier, and ran to the valley to seek help.

On July 15 about 0130, Popinchaulk contacted Ranger T. Kimbrough at Lupine Meadows, who in turn contacted the rescue coordinator, Ranger G. Montopli. Rangers D. Bywater and M. Vidak were immediately dispatched with first aid and rescue gear, while arrangements for a helicopter and additional Rangers were undertaken. Rangers Bywater and Vidak arrived on scene at 0645 and evaluated Steque. Lanny Johnson, P.A. (GTNP Medical Control), was contacted and advised of the situation. Because of his medical condition and location, the decision to short-haul Steque from his location to Lupine Meadows was finalized.

At 0740, the contract helicopter arrived at Lupine Meadows. Rangers T. Kimbrough, J. Springer, and R. Perch assisted with operations at Lupine Meadows. Ranger D. Burgette, S. Guenther, B. Weathermon, with emergency hire Lane Burgette, were flown to the Teton Glacier, along with USFS helicopter manager Holly Higgins, arriving about 0750 and 0805. Ranger L. Larson served as spotter for the operation. L. Burgette was assigned to A. Popinchaulk's son and friend, who were "noticeably affected" after witnessing the accident. As a result, the two were immediately flown to Lupine Meadows with their equipment.

After arriving at the scene (about 400 feet above the landing site on Teton Glacier), Burgette initiated an IV and administered Ancef as per L. Johnson's instructions. Ranger S. Guenther acted as on-scene incident commander. Along with spinal immobilization, Steque was immobilized in right lateral recumbent position onto the litter, and short-hauled directly to Lupine Meadows, arriving at 0936. He was then transferred to GTNP ambulance and taken to St. John's Hospital, where he was diagnosed with a fractured pelvis, fractured right thumb, and a significant laceration to his head that required sutures. (Source: George Montopoli, NPS Ranger, Grand Teton National Park)

Analysis

Mount Owen is a long climb, even if done over the course of two days. By the time one descends, unless in top physical condition, fatigue can play a significant role in what happens. (Source: Jed Williamson)

UNABLE TO FIND DESCENT ROUTE, DARKNESS
Wyoming, Grand Teton National Park, Grand Teton

On July 19 at 2105, I received a cell phone call via Teton Dispatch from John Rasmussen. Rasmussen stated that he and his wife were near the summit of the Grand Teton after having ascended the upper Exum Ridge, and were having difficulty locating the correct rappel point which allows direct access to the Upper Saddle and descent from the mountain. He also stated that he had only one 50-meter rope, and that his wife was suffering from mild hypothermia. I tried to figure out where they were located by asking a series of questions about what they could see from their position in the rapidly fading daylight. I was unable to determine their exact position and suggested that they prepare to spend the night where they were rather than attempt a tricky series of rappels at night. I received another call from Rasmussen about midnight saying that he and his wife were getting quite cold. I asked if they were shivering and he said that they were. I told him that was a good sign and that they should set up an anchor and clip into it for the night, and that I would check in with them at 0600.

When I spoke to Rasmussen at 0600 on the morning of the 20th, he stated that his wife was "very cold" and that they were "requesting assistance." I suggested that he set up a belay and attempt to climb around the corner and into the sunlight. I also relayed to Rasmussen that they were likely to encounter guided parties making their way down the Owen-Spalding pretty soon. Regarding assistance from the Park Service, I relayed to him that Ranger Jim Springer would be leaving the Lupine Meadows trailhead at 0700 on a regularly scheduled patrol in which he planned to ascend the Owen-Spalding and provide any assistance that he could. Later on in the mourning I learned that a Jackson Hole Mountain Guides party and an Exum party encountered the Rasmussens between the Pownall-Gilkey and Owen-Spalding routes and provided clothing and assistance in getting down the main rappel. Ranger Springer encountered the party near the "Eye of the Needle" as they were making their way down and they were moving along just fine at that point. (Source: Renny Jackson, NPS Ranger, Grand Teton National Park)

Analysis

This is one of those great incident reports because of what it *doesn't* say about the potential victims. The most important piece of information here, however, is to note that a night rescue was *not* set in motion. This was an appropriate call on the part of the ranger. It spared park personnel unnecessary person-hours and potential problems. (Source: Jed Williamson)

FALL ON ROCK—HAND-HOLD CAME LOOSE, CLIMBING UNROPED
Wyoming, Grand Teton National Park, Symmetry Spire

On July 28 about 1630, Mark Sachs (36) called Teton Dispatch (who transferred the call to rescue coordinator George Montopoli) using a cell phone borrowed from a hiker on the west shore of Jenny Lake. Sachs stated that his climbing partner, Laura Plaut (35) had fallen approximately 100 feet while scrambling unroped near the summit of Symmetry Spire. They had completed the Southwest Ridge route of Symmetry Spire earlier and were headed to the summit when the accident occurred. He said that she had a severe open fracture of her left elbow, a possible fractured left ankle, head lacerations, and other possible (internal) injuries (later confirmed at the hospital).

Contract helicopter 3HP was immediately requested and the rescue effort was initiated. Ranger J. Springer (spotter) flew an initial recon flight at 1700. Ranger A. Byerly then flew internally to Lake of the Crags. He reached Plaut at 1817 and rendered medical attention. Medical control Lanny Johnson, PA, was contacted. In addition to the injuries listed above, Plaut presented lower pack pain and was shivering from cold. Byerly immediately initiated full C-spine precautions, an IV, one gram of Ancef (at 1844) and heat pads. A decision was made to short-haul Plaut due to her injuries, lateness of the day, and potential injury to rescuers if other methods of evacuation were employed.

After immobilizing Plaut, she was short-hauled to Lupine Meadows Rescue Cache by 2017 and transferred to an ambulance. (Source: George Montopoli, NPS Ranger, Grand Teton National Park)

Analysis
Many who climb Symmetry Spire do the same thing Laura Plaut did for the final part of this climb. There have been many falls here. In this instance, the fall was probably caused because a hand-hold came away. Guides and even experienced climbers usually stay roped for the entire ascent. (Source: Jed Williamson)

RAPPEL FAILURE—ANCHOR CAME APART, INADEQUATE PROTECTION
Wyoming, Grand Teton National Park, Garnet Canyon
On September 15 about 1930, Julien Roques (20) fell 350 feet from the third pitch of the Open Book in Garnet Canyon. He sustained severe injuries during the fall resulting in his death.

Analysis
Upon investigation on the morning of September 17, it was noted that Roques was correctly attached to his rappel device and his fall initiated at the start of his rappel. Two descending rings were found attached to the rappel ropes near the victim. Since the descending rings were devoid of any part of the anchor system, investigating rangers assumed the anchor system failed on one side, allowing the descending rings to slide off the webbing or the webbing failed completely. The failed anchor system had to be at the location of their last rappel.

Rangers Jack McConnell and Leo Larson climbed two pitches of the Open Book route and located the failed anchor system. As suspected, part of the anchor system had failed, allowing the two descending rings to slide off the webbing. On closer inspection, the following was found: A short length of blue $\frac{9}{16}$-inch webbing had been knotted on *both ends* with a shorter length of red one inch tubular webbing threaded over it to act as a protective sheath. One knotted end of the $\frac{9}{16}$-inch webbing was inserted in a crack system that tapered down to about $\frac{1}{16}$-inch in width, allowing just enough space to thread the webbing through for about four inches. The other end of the $\frac{9}{16}$-inch blue webbing was looped back through the $\frac{1}{16}$-inch slot and the end knot wedged in the same crack system above. A short loop of the blue ⁹⁄₁₆-inch webbing with the red protective sheath and two descending rings were the complete anchor.

When Julien Roques and Mike Dollarhide (his partner) arrived at this *pre-rigged* anchor after their first rappel from the top of the Open Book, they inserted a camming device as a safety backup to the blue ⁹⁄₁₆-inch webbing anchor described above. Mike Dollarhide rappelled first on their 60-meter ropes and safely reached the bottom where they had started a few hours before. According to Dollarhide, the blue ⁹⁄₁₆-inch pre-rigged anchor held all his weight and that the back-up cam was not weighted. At this rappel, Roques and Dollarhide discussed pulling the safety back-up cam if the main anchor held well on Dollarhide's rappel. Mike Dollarhide started his rappel from the top of the flake *below* the anchor. This resulted in a directional downward pull. Since Dollarhide's rappel went well, the back-up cam was pulled by Roques. Roques then began his rappel and the fatal accident occurred.

Since Julien Roques was alone, his final actions at this rappel station will never be known. Based on evidence at the scene, Rangers Jack McConnell and Leo Larson came up with the following possible scenarios leading up to the catastrophic anchor failure:

(1) An end of this two-knot anchor simply failed after repeated use. This anchor was not inspected in detail either by Roques or Dollarhide. In fact, they thought the blue ⁹⁄₁₆-inch webbing completely *looped* through the rock and was tied with a water knot in the rear. It is possible the two end knots in the blue ⁹⁄₁₆-inch webbing were *stacked* in the crack system, allowing the top knot to slide over the top of the bottom knot and out of the crack system. (Note: The failed end was still knotted—the knot did not become undone.)

(2) The safety back-up cam was placed above the main anchor system. Roques would have had to climb up off the top of the flake to remove the anchor. If he started his rappel a little higher than Dollarhide, this would have resulted in a slight outward directional pull on the anchor, increasing its likelihood of failure.

(3) Julien Roques could have attached the ropes to his rappel device, climbed up to remove the back-up camming device, and then slipped. This would have shock-loaded the anchor, increasing its chance of failure.

It is ironic that this accident happened on a route that until very recently was walked off from the top. Only in the last couple years have some climbers opted to rappel this route. (Source: Leo Larson, NPS Ranger, Grand Teton National Park)

(Editor's Note: No reports from Devil's Tower were sent forward this year. After publication last year, a report of a fatality there came in from Kyle Dahm, who was climbing at the time of the incident. A middle aged man was descending after having been on the route Sundance with four others. He either rappelled off the end of his rope or fell while trying to scramble to a set of anchors for the final rappel.)

TABLE I
REPORTED MOUNTAINEERING ACCIDENTS

	Number of Accidents Reported		Total Persons Involved		Injured		Fatalities	
	USA	CAN	USA	CAN	USA	CAN	USA	CAN
1951	15		22		11		3	
1952	31		35		17		13	
1953	24		27		12		12	
1954	31		41		31		8	
1955	34		39		28		6	
1956	46		72		54		13	
1957	45		53		28		18	
1958	32		39		23		11	
1959	42	2	56	2	31	0	19	2
1960	47	4	64	12	37	8	19	4
1961	49	9	61	14	45	10	14	4
1962	71	1	90	1	64	0	19	1
1963	68	11	79	12	47	10	19	2
1964	53	11	65	16	44	10	14	3
1965	72	0	90	0	59	0	21	0
1966	67	7	80	9	52	6	16	3
1967	74	10	110	14	63	7	33	5
1968	70	13	87	19	43	12	27	5
1969	94	11	125	17	66	9	29	2
1970	129	11	174	11	88	5	15	5
1971	110	17	138	29	76	11	31	7
1972	141	29	184	42	98	17	49	13
1973	108	6	131	6	85	4	36	2
1974	96	7	177	50	75	1	26	5
1975	78	7	158	22	66	8	19	2
1976	137	16	303	31	210	9	53	6
1977	121	30	277	49	106	21	32	11
1978	118	17	221	19	85	6	42	10
1979	100	36	137	54	83	17	40	19
1980	191	29	295	85	124	26	33	8
1981	97	43	223	119	80	39	39	6
1982	140	48	305	126	120	43	24	14
1983	187	29	442	76	169	26	37	7
1984	182	26	459	63	174	15	26	6
1985	195	27	403	62	190	22	17	3
1986	203	31	406	80	182	25	37	14
1987	192	25	377	79	140	23	32	9
1988	156	18	288	44	155	18	24	4
1989	141	18	272	36	124	11	17	9
1990	136	25	245	50	125	24	24	4
1991	169	20	302	66	147	11	18	6
1992	175	17	351	45	144	11	43	6
1993	132	27	274	50	121	17	21	14

	Number of Accidents Reported		Total Persons Involved		Injured		Fatalities	
	USA	CAN	USA	CAN	USA	CAN	USA	CAN
1994	158	25	335	58	131	25	27	5
1995	168	24	353	50	134	18	37	7
1996	139	28	261	59	100	16	31	6
1997	158	35	323	87	148	24	31	13
1998	138	24	281	55	138	18	20	1
1999	123	29	248	69	91	20	17	10
2000	150	23	301	36	121	23	24	7
TOTALS	5225	778	9529	1639	4452	622	1219	266

TABLE II

	1951–1999			2000		
Geographical Districts	Number of Accidents	Deaths	Total Persons Involved	Number of Accidents	Deaths	Total Persons Involved
Canada						
Alberta	416	120	920	15	6	22
British Columbia	271	105	604	4	1	8
Yukon Territory	33	26	73	0	0	0
Ontario	35	9	64	1	0	1
Quebec	27	7	58	3	0	5
East Arctic	7	2	20	0	0	0
West Arctic	1	1	2	0	0	0
Practice Cliffs[1]	20	2	36	0	0	0
United States						
Alaska	413	160	648	16	3	28
Arizona, Nevada Texas	73	13	138	3	2	4
Atlantic–North	768	102	1302	16	1	30
Atlantic–South	74	21	140	6	2	12
California	1022	238	2122	50	6	109
Central	122	14	196	5	1	8
Colorado	650	188	1127	21	4	40
Montana, Idaho South Dakota	70	25	109	5	2	9
Oregon	149	73	362	3	1	5
Utah, New Mexico	120	41	216	7	0	16
Washington	947	278	720	11	1	26
Wyoming	491	108	907	7	1	14

[1]This category includes bouldering, artificial climbing walls, buildings, and so forth. These are also added to the count of each province, but not to the total count, though that error has been made in previous years. The Practice Cliffs category has been removed from the U.S. data.

TABLE III

	1951–99 USA	1959–99 CAN.	2000 USA	2000 CAN.
Terrain				
Rock	3759	455	85	11
Snow	2138	324	61	6
Ice	207	112	4	6
River	13	3	0	0
Unknown	22	8	0	0
Ascent or Descent				
Ascent	3345	483	93	18
Descent	2023	337	57	5
Unknown	247	5	0	0
Immediate Cause				
Fall or slip on rock	2611	245	67	8
Slip on snow or ice	844	171	30	7
Falling rock, ice, or object	523	118	14	4
Exceeding abilities	453	28	14	0
Avalanche	262	111	2	3
Exposure	241	13	2	0
Illness[1]	300	22	15	0
Stranded	280	40	8	0
Rappel Failure/Error[2]	228	40	9	1
Loss of control/glissade	171	16	11	0
Fall into crevasse/moat	141	44	4	0
Failure to follow route	134	28	8	0
Nut/chock pulled out	124	4	14	0
Piton/ice screw pulled out	87	12	0	0
Faulty use of crampons	74	5	4	0
Lightning	40	7	2	0
Skiing[3]	50	9	0	0
Ascending too fast	46	0	1	0
Equipment failure	11	2	0	0
Other[4]	269	32	19	0
Unknown	60	8	0	0
Contributory Causes				
Climbing unroped	919	153	15	2
Exceeding abilities	847	194	13	2
Inadequate equipment/clothing	567	75	19	0
Placed no/inadequate protection	553	79	27	5
Weather	400	58	9	0
Climbing alone	338	60	7	1
No hard hat	269	28	7	0
Nut/chock pulled out	189	17	5	0
Inadequate belay	144	22	8	2
Darkness	123	19	5	0
Poor position	126	15	9	3
Party separated	105	10	0	0
Piton/ice screw pulled out	84	10	1	1

	1951–99 USA	1959–99 CAN.	2000 USA	2000 CAN.
Contributory Causes, cont.				
Failure to test holds	80	19	1	3
Exposure	56	13	0	0
Failed to follow directions	68	11	1	0
Illness[1]	33	4	4	2
Equipment failure	10	7	1	0
Other[4]	239	85	4	5
Age of Individuals				
Under 15	117	12	1	0
15-20	1175	199	18	2
21-25	1199	236	26	2
26-30	1095	193	20	7
31-35	740	102	21	5
36-50	937	124	44	7
Over 50	154	22	8	1
Unknown	999	622	44	7
Experience Level				
None/Little	1554	291	39	1
Moderate (1 to 3 years)	1386	346	15	1
Experienced	1510	371	41	22
Unknown	1630	443	80	6
Month of Year				
January	193	16	3	2
February	184	41	2	2
March	256	55	5	1
April	349	29	12	3
May	762	50	20	1
June	912	59	29	2
July	962	230	23	1
August	905	155	26	4
September	1086	58	12	3
October	364	30	9	0
November	166	10	3	1
December	75	19	6	2
Unknown	12	1	0	0
Type of Injury/Illness (Data since 1984)				
Fracture	875	165	63	13
Laceration	476	59	29	4
Abrasion	240	65	10	3
Bruise	303	64	20	5
Sprain/strain	215	23	8	1
Concussion	163	20	11	1
Hypothermia	127	13	2	1
Frostbite	93	9	2	0
Dislocation	82	10	8	0
Puncture	30	5	3	4

	1951–99 USA	1959–99 CAN.	2000 USA	2000 CAN.
Type of Injury/Illness (Data since 1984), cont.				
Acute Mountain Sickness	23	0	4	0
HAPE	52	0	4	0
HACE	19	0	0	0
Other[5]	210	35	12	1
None	141	76	24	0

[1]These illnesses/injuries, which led directly to the accident, included: AMS (3), HAPE (4), exhaustion (3), ataxia, snow blindness, respiratory distress, acute abdomen, fatigue, dehydration, and hypothermia.

[2]This includes rappelling off the end of the rope, anchor(s) inadequate, lowering a climber (from above or below).

[3]This category was set up originally for ski mountaineering. Backcountry touring or snowshoeing incidents—even if one gets avalanched—are not included in the data

[4]These included: failure to turn back (5), hand-hold broke off (3), haste (4), improper haul-rope technique, improper tie-in, dislocated shoulder during self-arrest, old webbing broke when weighted, failure to disclose medical condition, webbing parted—ends held together by masking tape, high wind blew person over, slack in belay rope—wrapped around leader's leg and pulled him out of position, route underrated in guide book, anger and frustration.

[5]These included: pneumothorax (2), rope burns on hands (2), lightning burns (4), lost consciousness—lightning (3), exhaustion/fatigue (5), lost sensation in lower legs temporarily, collapsed lung, torn rotor-cuff, respiratory distress, acute abdomen, snow blindness, and ruptured kidney

(Editor's Note: Under the category "other," many of the particular items will have been recorded under a general category. For example, the climber who dislodges a rock that falls on another climber would be coded as Falling Rock/Object, or the climber who has a hand hold come loose and falls would also be coded as Fall On Rock.)

MOUNTAIN RESCUE UNITS IN NORTH AMERICA

**Denotes team fully certified—Technical Rock,
Snow & Ice, Wilderness Search;
S, R, SI = certified partially in Search, Rock, and/or Snow & Ice

ALASKA
ALASKA MOUNTAIN RESCUE GROUP. PO Box 241102, Anchorage,
AK 99524. www.amrg.org
DENALI NATIONAL PARK SAR. PO Box 588, Talkeetna, AK 99676
Dena_talkeetna@nps.gov
US ARMY ALASKAN WARFARE TRAINING CENTER. #2900 501 Second
St., APO AP 96508-2900

ARIZONA
APACHE RESCUE TEAM. PO Box 100, St. Johns, AZ 85936
ARIZONA DEPARTMENT OF PUBLIC SAFETY AIR RESCUE. Phoenix,
Flagstaff, Tucson, Kingman, AZ
ARIZONA DIVISION OF EMERGENCY SERVICES. Phoenix, AZ
GRAND CANYON NATIONAL PARK RESCUE TEAM. PO Box 129,
Grand Canyon, AZ 86023
****CENTRAL ARIZONA MOUNTAIN RESCUE TEAM/ MARICOPA
COUNTY SHERIFF'S OFFICE MR.** PO Box 4004 Phoenix, AZ 85030-4004.
www.mcsomr.org
SEDONA FIRE DISTRICT SPECIAL OPERATIONS RESCUE TEAM.
2860 Southwest Dr., Sedona, AZ 86336 ropes@sedona.net
****SOUTHERN ARIZONA RESCUE ASSN/ PIMA COUNTY SHERIFF'S
OFFICE.** PO Box 12892, Tucson, AZ 85732-2892.
http://hambox.theriver.com/sarci/sara01.html

CALIFORNIA
****ALTADENA MOUNTAIN RESCUE TEAM.** 780 E. Altadena Dr., Altadena,
CA 91001. www.altadenasheriffs.org/rescue/amrt.html
****BAY AREA MOUNTAIN RESCUE TEAM.** PO Box 19184, Stanford,
CA 94309. bamru@hooked.net
CALIFORNIA OFFICE OF EMERGENCY SERVICES. 2800 Meadowview
Rd., Sacramento, CA. 95832. warning.center@oes.ca.gov
****CHINA LAKE MOUNTAIN RESCUE GROUP.** PO Box 2037, Ridgecrest,
CA 93556. www.clmrg.org
****INYO COUNTY SHERIFF'S POSSE SAR.** PO Box 982, Bishop, CA 93514.
inyocosar@juno.com
JOSHUA TREE NATIONAL PARK SAR. 74485 National Monument Drive,
Twenty Nine Palms, CA 92277. patrick_suddath@nps.gov
****LOS PADRES SAR TEAM.** PO Box 6602, Santa Barbara, CA 93160-6602
****MALIBU MOUNTAIN RESCUE TEAM.** PO Box 222, Malibu, CA 90265.
www.mmrt.org
****MONTROSE SAR TEAM.** PO Box 404, Montrose, CA 91021.

RIVERSIDE MOUNTAIN RESCUE UNIT. PO Box 5444, Riverside, CA 92517. www.rmru.org   rmru@bigfoot.com
SAN BERNARDINO COUNTY SHERIFF'S CAVE RESCUE TEAM. 655 E. Third St. San Bernardino, CA 92415-0061. www.sbsd-vfu.org/units/SAR/SAR203/sar203_1.htm
SAN BERNARDINO COUNTY SO/ WEST VALLEY SAR. 13843 Peyton Dr., Chino Hills, CA 91709.
SAN DIEGO MOUNTAIN RESCUE TEAM. PO Box 81602, San Diego, CA 92138. www.sdmrt.org
SAN DIMAS MOUNTAIN RESCUE TEAM. PO Box 35, San Dimas, CA 91773.
SANTA CLARITA VALLEY SAR / L.A.S.O. 23740 Magic Mountain Parkway, Valencia, CA 91355. http://members.tripod.com/scvrescue/
SEQUOIA-KINGS CANYON NATIONAL PARK RESCUE TEAM. Three Rivers, CA 93271
SIERRA MADRE SAR. PO Box 24, Sierra Madre, CA 91025. www.mra.org/smsrt.html
VENTURA COUNTY SAR. 2101 E. Olson Rd, Thousand Oaks, CA 91362. www.vcsar.org
YOSEMITE NATIONAL PARK RESCUE TEAM. PO Box 577-SAR, Yosemite National Park, CA 95389

COLORADO
ALPINE RESCUE TEAM. PO Box 934, Evergreen, CO 80439. www.heart-beat-of-evergreen.com/alpine/alpine.html
COLORADO GROUND SAR. 2391 Ash St, Denver, CO 80222 www.coloradowingcap.org/CGSART/Default.htm
CRESTED BUTTE SAR. PO Box 485, Crested Butte, CO 81224
DOUGLAS COUNTY SEARCH AND RESCUE, PO Box 1102, Castle Rock, CO 80104.   www.dcsarco.org   info@dcsarco.org
EL PASO COUNTY SAR. 3950 Interpark Dr, Colorado Springs, CO 80907-9028. www.epcsar.org
ELDORADO CANYON STATE PARK. PO Box B, Eldorado Springs, CO 80025
GRAND COUNTY SAR. Box 172, Winter Park, CO 80482
LARIMER COUNTY SAR. 1303 N. Shields St., Fort Collins, CO 80524. www.fortnet.org/LCSAR/ lcsar@co.larimer.co.us
MOUNTAIN RESCUE ASPEN. 630 W. Main St, Aspen, CO 81611 www.mountainrescueaspen.org
PARK COUNTY SAR, CO. PO Box 721, Fairplay, CO 80440.
ROCKY MOUNTAIN NATIONAL PARK RESCUE TEAM. Estes Park, CO 80517
ROCKY MOUNTAIN RESCUE GROUP. PO Box Y, Boulder, CO 80306. www.colorado.edu/StudentGroups/rmrg/ rmrg@colorado.edu
ROUTT COUNTY SAR. PO Box 772837, Steamboat Springs, CO 80477 RCSAR@co.routt.co.us
SUMMIT COUNTY RESCUE GROUP. PO Box 1794, Breckenridge, CO 80424

**VAIL MOUNTAIN RESCUE GROUP. PO Box 1597, Vail, CO 81658. http://sites.netscape.net/vailmra/homepage   vmrg@vail.net
**WESTERN STATE COLLEGE MOUNTAIN RESCUE TEAM. Western State College Union, Gunnison, CO 81231. org_mrt@western.edu

IDAHO
**BONNEVILLE COUNTY SAR. 605 N. Capital Ave, Idaho Falls, ID 83402. www.srv.net/~jrcase/bcsar.html
**IDAHO MOUNTAIN SAR. PO Box 741, Boise, ID 83701. www.imsarv.org rsksearch@aol.com

MAINE
ACADIA NATIONAL PARK SAR. Bar Harbor, Maine

MARYLAND
**MARYLAND SAR GROUP. 5434 Vantage Point Road, Columbia, MD 21044. Peter McCabe@Ed.gov

MONTANA
GLACIER NATIONAL PARK SAR. PO Box 423, Glacier National Park, West Glacier, MT 59936
NORTHWEST MONTANA REGIONAL SAR ASSN. c/o Flat County SO, 800 S. Main, Kalispell, MT 59901
**WESTERN MONTANA MOUNTAIN RESCUE TEAM. University of Montana, University Center - Rm 105 Missoula, MT 59812

NEVADA
**LAS VEGAS METRO PD SAR. 4810 Las Vegas Blvd., South Las Vegas, NV 89119. www.lvmpdsar.com

NEW MEXICO
**ALBUQUERQUE MOUNTAIN RESCUE COUNCIL. PO Box 53396, Albuquerque, NM 87153. www.abq.com/amrc/ albrescu@swcp.com

NEW HAMPSHIRE
APPALACHIAN MOUNTAIN CLUB. Pinkham Notch Camp, Gorham, NH 03581
MOUNTAIN RESCUE SERVICE. PO Box 494, North Conway, NH 03860

NEW YORK
76 SAR. 243 Old Quarry Rd., Feura Bush, NY 12067
NY STATE FOREST RANGERS. 50 Wolf Rd., room 440C, Albany, NY 12233

OREGON
**CORVALLIS MOUNTAIN RESCUE UNIT. PO Box 116, Corvallis, OR 97339. www.cmrv.peak.org
(S, R) **DESCHUTES COUNTY SAR.** 63333 West Highway 20, Bend, OR 97701
**EUGENE MOUNTAIN RESCUE. PO Box 20, Eugene, OR 97440
**HOOD RIVER CRAG RATS RESCUE TEAM. 2880 Thomsen Rd., Hood River, OR 97031
**PORTLAND MOUNTAIN RESCUE. PO Box 5391, Portland, OR 97228. www.pmru.org info@pmru.org

PENNSYLVANNIA
**ALLEGHENY MOUNTAIN RESCUE GROUP. c/o Mercy Hospital, 1400 Locust, Pittsburgh, PA 15219-5166. www.asrc.net/amrg
**WILDERNESS EMERGENCY STRIKE TEAM. 11 North Duke Street, Lancaster, PA 17602. www.west610.org

UTAH
**DAVIS COUNTY SHERIFF'S SAR. PO Box 800, Farmington, UT 84025. www.dcsar.org
ROCKY MOUNTAIN RESCUE DOGS. 3353 S. Main #122, Salt Lake City, UT 84115
**SALT LAKE COUNTY SHERIFF'S SAR. 4474 South Main St., Murray, UT 84107
SAN JUAN COUNTY EMERGENCY SERVICES. PO Box 9, Monticello, UT 84539
**UTAH COUNTY SHERRIF'S SAR. PO Box 330, Provo, UT 84603-0330. ucsar@utah.uswest.net
**WEBER COUNTY SHERIFF'S MOUNTAIN RESCUE. 745 Nancy Dr, Ogden, UT 84403. http://planet.weber.edu/mru
ZION NATIONAL PARK SAR. Springdale, UT 84767

VERMONT
**STOWE HAZARDOUS TERRAIN EVACUATION. P.O. Box 291, Stowe, VT 05672. www.stowevt.org/htt/

VIRGINIA
AIR FORCE RESCUE COORDINATION CENTER. Suite 101, 205 Dodd Building, Langley AFB, VA 23665-2789. www2.acc.af.mil/afrcc/ airforce.rescue@usa.net

WASHINGTON STATE
**BELLINGHAM MOUNTAIN RESCUE COUNCIL. PO Box 292, Bellingham, WA 98225
**CENTRAL WASHINGTON MOUNTAIN RESCUE COUNCIL. PO Box 2663, Yakima, WA 98907. www.nwinfo.net/~cwmr/ cwmr@nwinfo.net

**EVERETT MOUNTAIN RESCUE UNIT. PO Box 2566, Everett, WA 98203. emrui@aol.com

MOUNT RAINIER NATIONAL PARK RESCUE TEAM. Longmire, WA 98397

NORTH CASCADES NATIONAL PARK RESCUE TEAM. 728 Ranger Station Rd, Marblemount, WA 98267

**OLYMPIC MOUNTAIN RESCUE. PO Box 4244, Bremerton, WA 98312. www.olympicmountainrescue.org information@olympicmountainrescue.org

OLYMPIC NATIONAL PARK RESCUE TEAM. 600 Park Ave, Port Angeles, WA 98362

**SEATTLE MOUNTAIN RESCUE. PO Box 67, Seattle, WA 98111. www.eskimo.com/~pc22/SMR/smr.html

**SKAGIT MOUNTAIN RESCUE. PO Box 2, Mt. Vernon, WA 98273

**TACOMA MOUNTAIN RESCUE. PO Box 696, Tacoma, WA 98401. www.tmru.org

NORTH COUNTRY VOLCANO RESCUE TEAM. 404 S. Parcel Ave, Yacolt, WA 98675. www.northcountryems.org/vrt/index.html

WASHINGTON, DC

NATIONAL PARK SERVICE, EMS/SAR DIVISION. Washington, DC

US PARK POLICE AVIATION. Washington, DC

WYOMING

GRAND TETON NATIONAL PARK RESCUE TEAM. PO Box 67, Moose, WY 83012

PARK COUNTY SAR, WY. Park County SO, 1131 11th, Cody, WY 82412

CANADA

NORTH SHORE RESCUE TEAM. 165 E. 13th St, North Vancouver, B.C., Canada V7L 2L3

**ROCKY MOUNTAIN HOUSE SAR. Box 1888, Rocky Mountain House, Alberta, Canada T0M 1T0

MOUNTAIN RESCUE ASSOCIATION

c/o PO Box 501
Poway, CA 92074 USA
www.mra.org

Rocky Henderson, President
Portland Mountain Rescue, OR
rockyh9@earthlink.net

Monty Bell, Vice President
San Diego Mountain Rescue Team, CA
mbell@newwaypro.com

Kayley Trujillo, Secretary/Treasurer
San Diego Mountain Rescue Team, CA
kayley@splitinfinity.com

Gary Banks, Member at Large
Salt Lake County Sheriff's SAR, UT

Yvette Choma, Member at Large
Rocky Mountain House SAR, Alberta, CAN

Tim Kovacs, Public Affairs Director
Central AZ MRA/MCSO MR, AZ
tkovacs@goodnet.com